AF669496

ISLAMIC ETIQUETTE

ERKAM PUBLICATIONS

ISLAMIC ETIQUETTE

Faruk KANGER - Lokman HELVACI

Original Title: Âdâb-ı Muâşeret
Author: Faruk Kanger
Lokman Helvacı
Translator: İsmail Eriş
Editor: İsmail Eriş
Coordinator: Adem Özdemir
Graphics: Rasim Şakiroğlu

Address: Ikitelli Organize Sanayi Bölgesi
Mah. Atatürk Bulvarı, Haseyad
1. Kısım No: 60/3-C Başakşehir,
Istanbul, Turkey
Tel: (90-212) 671-0700 pbx
Fax: (90-212) 671-0748
E-mail: info@islamicpublishing.org
Web site: www.islamicpublishing.org
Language: English

ERKAM PUBLICATIONS

بسم الله الرحمن الرحيم

İstanbul - 2021

CONTENTS

ISLAMIC ETIQUETTE

RULES OF MANNERS AND COURTESY

Allah, glory unto Him, created us in the best appearance, with a pure heart. He has placed in us an advanced intellect and a delicate conscience. He placed us in the trust of our parents so that they can educate us to be nice people with good character. Allah, glory unto him, has furthermore sent prophets and books and through them invites us to His Paradise. He wants us to return to Paradise, to the purest and most exceptional form of life, in a character that is worthy of that purity. He expects us to be delicate and sensitive Muslims with good manners.

After true faith, deeds of worship offered purely for the sake of the Almighty and observing what is permissible and impermissible, there come the principles of morality commanded by our Lord. There are further points of sensitivity and elegance within these general moral principles which we call manners. Manifesting these sensitivities and courtesy to other members of society is called "etiquette (Adāb al-Muasharah) or good manners".

Etiquette (Adāb al-Muasharah) is exceptionally important in the Islamic civilization; for the principles of 'loving the created for the sake of the Creator (to love each being created by Allah, glory unto Him, for the reason that each is a unique work of His art) and 'looking onto creation with the gaze of the Lord' (to value each created being as they are valued by the Lord Himself) have been deeply imprinted onto our hearts and minds.

Mawlana Rumi describes just how important etiquette are for us:

"Etiquette is what separates human beings from animals. Open your eyes and see: All of the Lord's words and each verse of the Qur'an explain nothing but good manners. The greatest wealth that man can have are knowledge and manners. Manners never grow old, decay or perish!"

A poet says:

Manners…a God-given crown,
Wear it lest in troubles you drown

Some further words of wisdom regarding manners are:

"Let your words be sweet and elegant. A rude man is like a wild dog that gets stoned by everyone."

"A man without manners is nothing short of a donkey…even if he be knowledgeable."

(Even if a person is wise enough to carry the knowledge of books in his mind; If he lacks the sense of decency and modesty that distinguishes him from an animal, he is no different than a donkey carrying a book on his back.)

Good manners are the most precious provisions of the traveler of the Truth. A person cannot be both pious and at the same time rude, quarrelsome and inconsiderate. Because in terms of its spirit, the essence of Islam is tawhid in creed, and good manners, following the straight path and mercy in deeds. In this respect, it can be said that Islam, with all its fundamental principles, is a religion of total politeness, grace and refinement, that is, "good manners".

The first of the most important good manner for a servant is:

GOOD MANNERS TOWARDS ALLAH ALMIGHTY

It should not be forgotten that Satan was expelled from the Divine Presence, not because of his lack of knowledge or practice, but because of his lack of good manners. Therefore, the best virtue to fight against Satan is to have good manners. Mawlana Rumi explains this as follows: "When Satan – May Allah's curse be upon him- did not prostrate to Adam and disobeyed Allah's command, he said:

"My essence is of fire, while his is of mud. How is it appropriate for the superior one to prostrate to the inferior one?'" Because of this unmannerly response to Allah Almighty, Satan was cursed and was expelled from the divine presence. Moreover, he acted arrogantly and tried to argue with the One who created him."

The servant, who acts with good manners towards Allah Almighty avoids indecent actions; in this way, he becomes aware of his faults, mistakes and heedlessness in his acts of worship and daily relations. He does not suffer from the disease of trusting his deeds.

We must not forget that Allah the Most High is always with us. A believer's goal is to achieve the "sense of ihsan", that is to say, the sense of realizing that he is always in the presence of Allah, and trying to act both externally and internally with good manners towards Allah.

The second greatest manners, after the good manners towards Allah, is the good manners towards the Messenger of Allah – upon him blessings and peace -.

GOOD MANNERS TOWARDS OUR PROPHET

The Companions – May Allah be well-pleased with them- manifested the most perfect examples of the respect and good manners that one must show towards the Messenger of Allah – upon him blessings and peace -. In this regard, they defined their state of awe and decency when they were in the presence of the Prophet: "As if there was a bird on our head and we were afraid that it would fly away if we moved."

The manners of the Companions towards the Messenger of Allah – upon him blessings and peace - were to such a degree that they, most of the time, considered it an indecency to even ask him a question. For this reason, they would even hope if a Bedouin from the desert would come and ask questions and thus, they would too be blessed with the conversation of the Prophet – upon him blessings and peace -.

On the other hand, to send peace and blessings whenever the name of the Messenger of Allah – upon him blessings and peace - is mentioned is one of the good manners commanded by Allah Almighty to us as Muslim nation. It is stated in the Qur'an:

"Allah and His angels send blessings on the Prophet: O you that believe! Send you blessings on him, and salute him with all respect." (al-Ahzab, 33: 56)

"(O believers!) Deem not the summons of the Messenger among yourselves like the summons of one of you to another..." (al-Nur, 24: 63)

Ibn Abbas – May Allah be well-pleased with him - said about this verse:

"People used to address the Messenger of Allah as "O Muhammad, O Abu al-Qasim". In order to glo-

rify the honor of His Messenger, Allah Almighty forbade them from addressing him like that.

After the revelation of this verse, people started to address him, "O Prophet of Allah, O Messenger of Allah!" (Abu Nuaym, Dalail, I, 46)

Therefore, mentioning the Prophet – upon him blessings and peace - only by his name is contrary to the good morals of being a member of his ummah. Along with his blessed name, his lofty and holy qualities should also be pronounced. In addition, it is necessary to show good manners and courtesy towards everything that is close to the Messenger of Allah – upon him blessings and peace - .

Another of most important rule of manners for a believer is the good manners that should be shown towards his Holy Book.

SHOWING GOOD MANNERS AND GRATIFICATION TOWARDS THE HOLY QUR'AN

The Qur'an is the last and supreme divine book. It is a manifestation of Allah Almighty's attribute of speech. In many verses, the lofty attributes of the Holy Qur'an are mentioned. Some of them are as follows:

"And We have bestowed upon you the Seven Oft-repeated (verses) and the Grand Qur'an." (al-Hijr, 15: 87)

"Qaf: By the Glorious Qur'an!" (Qaf, 50: 1)

"And verily, it (the Qur'an) is in the Mother of the Book, in Our Presence, high (in dignity), full of wisdom." (al-Zukhruf, 43: 4)

The Holy Qur'an is one of the symbols of Allah. Allah Almighty orders us to avoid disrespecting these symbols He has placed on the earth. (al-Maida, 5: 2.) He states that those who honor and respect them will achieve goodness. The following is stated in verses:

"Such (is the Pilgrimage): whoever honors the sacred rites of Allah, for him it is good in the Sight of his Lord..." (al-Hajj, 22: 30)

"Such (is his state): and whoever holds in honor the symbols of Allah, such (honor) should come truly from piety of heart." (al-Hajj, 22: 32)

The first condition of making good use of the Qur'an is to approach it with a sense of decency and respect. Because this state of respect is a manifestation of the importance attributed to the Qur'an.

In showing respect to the Qur'an, we can mention the following:

- In order to honor the Qur'an, one should not keep it below the waist level.

- While reading, he should hold it close to his chest or place it on anything in front of him, not on the ground.

- Likewise, he should not leave the Qur'an open or place any books or objects on it. The Qur'an must always be above all other books.

- He should not enter places where there is impurity such as toilets and bathrooms, and he should not read the Qur'an there.

- Likewise, he should not read the Qur'an when he is sleepy and he is not aware what he is saying.

- One should not pass a day without looking at the Holy Qur'an at least once.

- One should not recite the Qur'an in markets, in places where there is noise, in inappropriate places where vain business is carried out.

- The verses of the Holy Qur'an should not be written on inappropriate places.

- When writing them on a suitable place, it should not be written with incomplete, small and bad-looking calligraphy.

- When talking about the Qur'an and its verses, one should always speak respectfully.

- If it is dusty, it should be cleaned immediately.

- A paper on which the word of Allah and His Messenger is written should not be used to wrap food or anything else, such papers should not be torn and thrown away, and if they need to be destroyed, they should be burned or buried in a clean soil at a remote place.

- One should not lay down extending his feet in the direction of the Qur'an.

GOOD MANNERS BETWEEN PARENTS AND CHILDREN

Showing respect to the rights of parents is one of the most important principles of etiquette. Serving them, talking them with good words and kindness, especially when they get old, is the parents' one of the greatest rights upon their children. Loving parents and service them is commanded in the Qur'an after worshiping Allah. Allah Almighty says:

"Your Lord has decreed that you worship none but Him, and that you be kind to parents. Whether one or both of them attain old age in your life, say not to them a word of contempt, nor repel them, but address them in terms of honor."

"And, out of kindness, lower to them the wing of humility, and say: "My Lord! bestow on them Your Mercy even as they cherished me in childhood."" (al-Isra, 17: 23-24)

Ali's - May Allah be well-pleased with him - mother, Fatima bint Asad - May Allah be well-pleased with her - served the Prophet – upon him blessings and peace - in his youth as if she were his real mother. When this pious woman died, the Messenger of Allah

– upon him blessings and peace - went to her funeral, sat by her bedside, and witnessed her loyalty and service in the presence of Allah and said:

"O my mother! may Allah have mercy on you. You were my mother after my (own) mother. You would not eat but feed me, you would not wear yourself, but you would clothe me, you would feed me good foods by depriving yourself from them, and while you were doing these, you would desire only the pleasure of Allah and the life in the hereafter."

Again, a man came to the Prophet and asked:

"Who among the people is most deserving of a fine treatment from my hand?" He said: "Your mother." He again said: Then who (is the next one)? He said: "Again it is your mother (who deserves the best treatment from you)." He said: "Then who (is the next one)?" He (the Holy Prophet) said: "Again, it is your mother." He (again) said: "Then who?" Thereupon he said: "Then it is your father." (See Muslim, Birr, 2)

In other words, Allah's Messenger – upon him blessings and peace - expresses the sacrifices done by the mother, of course, by the father as well.

"Father (as narrated by al-Tirmidhi) is the middle gate of Paradise." (al-Tirmidhi, Birr, 3, [1901])

The most important one among the other people's rights is the right of parents. Obedience to parents comes next after obedience to Allah and His Messenger. Because our parents are our reason for existence and our benefactor. They are exceptional monuments of virtue that build our material and spiritual lives. A mother's heart and enfolding arms with love are a magnificent classroom where a child is nurtured. The home is the first educational institution that shapes the child's future. Therefore, the parents' rights over their children are too numerous to count.

Virtuous parents are a great mercy and blessing for the children. A righteous mother is like a bosom of mercy bestowed on human beings by Divine Power, a source of happiness in the family, the light of peace and purity, and a fountain of compassion for family members. It is an exceptional and glorious manifestation of our Lord's names "al-Rahman (The Most or Entirely Merciful)" and "al-Rahim (The Bestower of Mercy)" in the world.

The rights of the parents over their children are so great that it is very difficult, even impossible, to repay for them. The following simile draws attention to this in a hadith:

"A son does not repay what he owes his father unless he buys him (the father) in case he is a slave and then emancipates him." (Muslim, Itq, 25; Abu Dawud, Adab, 119-120; al-Tirmidhi, Birr, 8/1906)

For this reason, if any good and kindness is to be done for the sake of Allah, it is necessary to think about the parents first. Then other people from the closest to the farthest... The following is stated in a verse:

"...Whatever you spend that is good, is for parents and kindred and orphans and those in want and for wayfarers. And whatever you do that is good, -Allah knows it well." (al-Baqara, 2: 215)

In the subject of raising children with good manners, we can summarize the main issues that parents should pay particular attention to as follows:

a) A good name should be given to the child that will spirituality inspire the child. The first of the rights of the child over the parents is that they give him/her a "beautiful name".

b) Attention should be paid to the "halal"ness of the morsels that are fed to the children in order for the children to grow up in a favorable environment.

c) Children's behavior should always be "controlled" without making them feel it.

e) Good deeds of children should be "appreciated" and rewarded, and their mistakes should not be ignored.

Because positive behaviors are reinforced with rewards and make a permanent place in the personality of the child.

f) The child should not be forced to be insolent by frequent punishment.

g) While teaching orders, prohibitions and rules, they should be persuaded by explaining their reasons "in a way that they can understand".

h) Good manners (modes of behavior) and "ethical principles" should be taught, especially wealthy families should prevent their children from being rude and arrogant to their peers. Because such behaviors become habits over time. They should always be inculcated with modesty and humility.

ı) Children should be reminded of Allah's blessings and should be accustomed to "praise and gratitude. By giving examples from the life of our Prophet -upon him blessings and peace-, efforts should be made to shape the children's inner worlds in a spiritual climate.

j) At a young age, he should be "accustomed to worship and service", and the responsibility of worship and the importance of service should be inculcated to them.

In short, if we want our child to be perfect, we must strive to be perfect parents.

No other being has been created that can share the love and respect shown to our mothers, who carry us first in their wombs, then in their arms, and in their hearts until they die. Mothers, who take upon the responsibility of housewifery and child upbringing on their shoulders, are worthy of deep affection, deep respect and a lifetime of gratitude.

Is there a measure that can determine the limits of the immense compassion that accumulates in a mother's soul? They feed us but do not eat themselves, dress us but forget their own clothes, or help us sleep, but deprive themselves from sleeping... Is it possible to pay the rights of the mothers and fathers who give their entire existence so that no dust would touch upon us in the storms of life? How beautifully Mawlana Rumi expresses:

"Watch out for your mother's right! Crown him on your head! For, if mothers had not gone into labor, children would not have found a way to be born."

PERSONAL HYGIENE

Allah, glory unto Him, is clean and loves those who are clean.

Our Lord has created His servants as clean as they can ever be. When a baby is born, everyone desires to take the baby in their arms, kiss and smell him. Man is born into the world with purity and innocence; for he has been created pure, both physically and spiritually. And as human beings, we must therefore protect that state of spiritual and physical purity. The Beloved Prophet –upon him blessings and peace- informs us of this need when he says:

"Surely Allah is good and beautiful; and He loves that which is good and beautiful. He is clean and loves cleanliness." (al-Tirmidhi, Adab, 41) and *"Cleanliness is one half of faith."* (Muslim, Taharah, 1).

The Blessed Prophet –upon him blessings and peace- was one day speaking to his Companions when a man with messy hair and untidy clothes entered the scene. His appearance struck the attention of everyone there. Suddenly, all eyes were fixed on him. The Messenger of Allah –upon him blessings and peace- certainly could not approve of a Muslim looking like that.

His expression became a little serious. He did not like what he saw.

It was clear that the man was seeking permission to join the talk. Without making it obvious to the others, the Blessed Prophet –upon him blessings and peace- made a polite gesture to the man, signaling him to fix up his hair and clothes. The man understood and left immediately. Before too long, he came back once again, this time with his hair combed and clothes tidied. Seeing the man neatened, the Blessed Prophet –upon him blessings and peace- smiled. He invited him and changed the subject of his talk to personal hygiene and tidiness. To indicate to the man that how he looked now was much better than how he previously looked, the Beloved Messenger –upon him blessings and peace- said:

"Is it not better for one to be clean, neat and nicely appearing than to be untidy with devilishly unkempt hair?" (Muwattaa, Sha'ar, 7)

The Beloved Prophet –upon him blessings and peace- says:

"Surely Allah is good and beautiful; and He loves that which is good and beautiful. He is clean and loves cleanliness." (al-Tirmidhi, Adab, 41)

"Cleanliness is one half of faith." (Muslim, Taharah, 1).

How do we Maintain Our Personal Hygiene?

❖ On waking up in the morning, our first cleansing activity should be performing ablution for the first ritual prayer of the day. Ablution is a way of cleansing not only physically but also spiritually.

❖ We must wash and comb our hair several times a week. Our hair should always smell nice. It is also a nice habit for a person to carry a comb and mirror with him.

❖ While performing ablution, we must thoroughly clean the insides of our ears. Our ears must not look dirty.

❖ We must thoroughly clean our noses, especially while performing ablution. There should not remain any boogers, either dry or moist.

❖ We must brush our teeth using miswak, or a toothbrush and toothpaste and even dental floss if need be. Miswak helps clean our teeth and makes them appear shiny. It is also good for the gums.

Before the advent of Islam, people had not even the slightest awareness of dental hygiene and health. Islam thus revolutionized dental care. The Beloved Prophet –upon him blessings and peace- used to place great emphasis on dental hygiene. He would advice his Companions saying:

- "I know that you find it difficult to regularly clean your teeth. Yet dental hygiene is so important for your health that had I not known that it would not be too troublesome for you, I would certainly have commanded you to brush your teeth with miswak at the time of each ritual prayer." (Source: al-Bukhari, Juma, 8; al-Tirmidhi, Taharah, 18) For I clean my teeth before each ritual prayer and every time I wake up." (Source: Muslim, Musafirin, 139)

Men should keep their hair cut and neat and trim their beards and moustaches, if they have any. The Beloved Prophet –upon him blessings and peace- used to tidy his hair and beard by looking at a water-filled container as mirror.

When we come home in the evening, we must thoroughly wash our hands until our fingers and nails are properly cleaned.

Those who work in labor jobs, if needed, should bathe or take a shower when they come home in the evening.

Pubic and underarm hair should be shaved at least once a week or twice a month. Otherwise, the smell would make others uncomfortable.

The fingernails and toenails should be cut at least twice a month.

The Beloved Prophet –upon him blessings and peace- once said to Ali – May Allah be well-pleased with him-, "Cut your nails, O Ali; for the harmful creatures (micro organisms) gather under long nails."

A Muslim is someone who shines both inwardly and outwardly.

A Muslim ought to be healthy, strong and vigorous; for he must be an exemplary person. He represents what a beautiful religion Islam is through his health, energy, cleanliness and inner peace. All people should look upon a Muslim with envy and admiration and get an idea as to what kind of a human being the Blessed Prophet –upon him blessings and peace- was.

AS IF ABOUT TO ENTER THE DIVINE PRESENCE… (A STORY)

The Battle of Gallipoli marks a legendary feat of heroism shown by the Turks against their enemies who attacked on their religion, homeland and sacred values.

Colonel Cevdet Pasha, who was present on the battlefield, recounts:

"My brave men fought courageously today, from dawn until sunset. Towards sunset, I took a walk between their ranks to inspect how they were doing.

From a distance, I saw certain white marks which I could not make out clearly at the time. The night had slowly begun to cave in; therefore, I could not properly recognize the things I was seeing. I called my watchman and asked him.

'What are those white marks I see from a distance, son?'

'I will go and find out right away, sir', he said.

It was not long before he returned and began to explain. However, as he spoke, his voice sounded husky, as if he was trying to knock back his tears:

'Sir, our unit stationed over there', he said, 'has been in the thick of some fierce combat in the past few days. Most of them have already been martyred. The few who have managed to survive just know that it is only a matter of time before they are martyred themselves. They said to me, *'Allah-willing, when we are martyred tomorrow, we do not wish to enter the presence of our Lord and His Messenger with dirty clothes. We have hence washed our clothes and hung them up to dry'* The watchman continued:

'They will take their clothes off the lines as soon as they are dried, sir…'

Before he could even finish his last sentence, the watchman finally let go of all the tears he had been struggling to hold back up until then. Tears began rolling down his check like waterfall…"

It was this pure spirit that granted Muslims victory at Gallipoli.

TOILET MANNERS

Relief in the toilet is a comfort and reason for thanking the Lord.

The Almighty, who created His servants, has provided them the ways of ease and comfort for them to meet all their needs. The following story alone is enough to illustrate us how thankful we should be over the comfort of being able to find relief in the toilet.

The story goes that a sultan asks one of his viziers, renowned for his wisdom and intellect:

'What is one thing on earth that gives man the greatest comfort?'

'Relief in the toilet', answers the vizier. Unhappy with the answer, the sultan sends the vizier away.

Sometime later, the sultan becomes constipated. So intense was his constipation that he could not even manage to urinate. With his stomach swollen like a drum and almost about to explode, he finds himself in unbearable pain. He takes all the medication given by the doctor but to no avail. Then suddenly, he remembers the words of his vizier.

'How right he was', he says to himself and calls the vizier once again.

'I beg you to pray for me…and find me a cure so that I am saved from this pain', he says.

'I will pray for you, my sultan, and find you a cure', says the vizier, 'only on the condition that you give me half your treasures if you indeed do end up being cured.'

Helpless, the sultan accepts the vizier's deal; after all, what good was there in wealth without health? The vizier then prays for the sultan and hands him some medicine. A short time later, the sultan finds himself cured and once again able to go to the toilet.

Thanking the vizier, the sultan then hands him the keys of one half of his treasures as promised. But the wise vizier simply looks at the sultan and says:

'What kind of a treasure is this, my sultan, that it can be traded for just a relief in the toilet? I am in no need of such a treasure…you can have it all!'

Indeed, to give us a lesson of wisdom, each time the Beloved Prophet –upon him blessings and peace- went to the toilet, he would say beforehand:

اَللّٰهُمَّ اِنِّى اَعُوذُ بِكَ مِنَ الْخُبْثِ وَالْخَبَائِثِ

Allahumma inni audhu bika mina'l-khubthi wa'l-khabaith

'O Allah! I seek refuge with You from the wicked and noxious things.' (Muslim, Hayd, 122)

And when he came out of the privy, he would pray saying:

اَلْحَمْدُ لِلّٰهِ الَّذِى أَذْهَبَ عَنِّى الأَذَى وَعَافَانِى

Alhamdu'li-llahi'lladhi adhhaba anni'l-adha wa afani

'Praise be to Allah who has removed harm from me and kept me in health.' (Ibn Majah, Taharah, 10)

What should we pay attention to in the toilet?

Toilet hygiene is directly related to cleanliness of both the body and the clothes. It is therefore very important.

While entering the toilet, we should not have anything on us that have pieces from the Holy Qur'an written on it.

When entering and exiting the toilet, we should read the prayers that the Beloved Prophet –upon him blessings and peace- has taught us.

We should enter the toilet with the left foot and exit it with the right.

We must not urinate whilst standing. That is harmful for our health and hygiene. Instead, we should crouch while relieving ourselves.

One must not read anything, speak, sing, whistle, say or respond to a greeting and mention the name of Allah whilst in the toilet. One should exit immediately once done.

In a situation where it is necessary to see to the need in the outdoors, one must find a place remote from people and cover up as much as possible. One must neither face nor turn his back towards the direction of Qiblah while relieving himself.

When it becomes necessary to see to the need in the outdoors, one must prefer spots that people are least likely to walk pass.

One must refrain from things like spitting or blowing the noise inside the toilet that will put off people who come afterwards. We must leave the toilet in the condition that we ourselves would like to find it; even if that might not actually be the condition we have found it in the first place.

How do we wash up in the toilet *(taharah)*?

Cleaning the private parts in the toilet should be performed with the left hand,

If possible, it is better to first wipe the area with a dry toilet paper, wash the area with water and then once again dry it with toilet paper.

Men first perform *taharah* after urination by squeezing their private parts with their middle and index fingers from bottom to top to be sure nothing left in it. After defecating, they perform *taharah* by using their middle, ring and little fingers by wiping their private parts from front to back.

Women perform *taharah* by using their middle, ring and little fingers and wipe their private parts from the front to back.

To maintain hygiene inside the toilet, one should only use to right hand to make contact with things that are used jointly by everyone like the door handle, the tap, the plastic pot, the toilet paper and flush.

If one is relieving in place where there is no water or toilet paper, then he should use leaves or a suitable piece of stone for cleansing.

After leaving the privy, the hands must be thoroughly washed preferably with soap.

After stepping out of the toilet, men should wait for a few minutes as a precaution against any urine trickles. After moving about awhile, they proceed to perform ablution. In this regard women should also take similar precautions.

An idolater once mockingly said to Salman al-Farisi –May Allah be well-pleased with him-,

“I hear that your friend Muhammad teaches you everything…even the way you are supposed to crouch in the toilet!”

Salman Farisi –May Allah be well-pleased with him- replied with a serious tone:

"Yes, indeed. He teaches us the finest rules of manners and hygiene". He then began to explain to the idolater the Prophet's –upon him blessings and peace- advices regarding the appropriate toilet manners. (Muslim, Taharah, 57-58)

BATHROOM MANNERS

A Muslim is born clean, lives clean and dies clean.

Man comes into this world clean, both physically and spiritually. A newborn is immediately washed and wrapped in a bundle the moment he is born. Babies are so pure and innocent that everyone naturally feels like smelling and kissing them. Until they can bathe on their own, babies and children are washed by their parents. As they grow older, they begin to take care of the task by themselves. And when there comes a day when they die like every human being, they are again thoroughly washed and wrapped in a shroud by their loved ones, just like the bundle they had once been wrapped in at the time of their birth. And with compassion, they are laid to rest in earth, like the arms of their mother.

What should be paid attention when cleaning the body in the bathroom?

One must bathe or take a shower at least once a week (and even more if need be).

One must do so indoors, in a place where nobody can see.

In public baths or Turkish baths which are open to public use, one must cover certain parts of their body and not expose them to others.

For males, the limits of the body that must be covered before others is the area from the bellybutton to the just underneath the kneecaps, while for females, it is the area from the breasts to just underneath the kneecaps.

One must not look at the covered parts of other people's body in baths open to public use.

One must enter the bathroom by saying the statement of *'audhu basmalah'* and the above-mentioned supplication said while entering the toilet and then proceed to enter with the left foot.

Before entering the bathroom, one should say supplications along the lines of, 'O Lord! Purify my soul from the dirt of sins and immorality, just as you cleanse my body from the dirt.'

Harun Rashid, a Muslim caliph famous for his sense of justice, one day accidentally poured boiling hot water on himself while bathing. He ran out from the Turkish bath in pain. His back was severely burnt. The pain lasted for days. After that day, he gave charity to hundreds of needy persons.

Later on, he would always remind his friends of that painful day and reflect,

"In this life, I cannot even stand hot water that will only purify me of my dirt. What is to become of me in the Hereafter if I end up being sent to Hellfire over the dirt of my sins?"

We must bathe or shower in the most beautiful spiritual feelings and thank our Lord: for He who creates each creation in the manner He pleases, could easily have created each of us as a stray dog that never gets to bathe itself!

While bathing or taking a shower, we must not sing or even speak unless we have to.

We must cover the parts of our body that need to be covered to the best of ability, for this is a practice of the Blessed Prophet –upon him blessings and peace-.

We should perform major ablution (ghusl) with each shower, even this is not obligatory. That way, we will also gain spiritual rewards for performing an act of worship.

For a thorough cleaning, we should use a soap and washcloth.

We should always begin washing our body from top to bottom; for instance, begin from the head and shoulders and then move down, always giving priority to the right limbs before the left ones (such as ear, shoulder, arm, foot etc.).

We leave the bathroom with our right foot and say the above-mentioned prayer said when leaving the toilet.

We must not leave behind any dirt or rubbish and ventilate the bathroom while we are leaving.

We then leave the bathroom in gratitude to Allah, glory unto Him, for giving us the blessing of cleanliness.

Physical and spiritual purity are two parts of a whole.

Allah, glory unto Him, has prescribed to be in a state of minor (wudu) and major ablution (ghusl) before reading the Qur'an and offering ritual prayer. As a matter of fact, these forms of purification have the aim of purifying our hearts from the dirt of sin and evil. There was a sign at the entrance of a Turkish bath in old Istanbul that read:

If you are a man of bad habits and a rotten character

Do not expect the hamam to cleanse you!

If you want a true purification, clean your heart first and then your body...

Muslims have an astonishing sense of manners and hygiene!

With a sensitive sense of manners and hygiene, Muslims have, throughout history, earned the praises and admiration of even non-Muslims. One of them was Dr. A. Brayer who, after travelling many Ottoman towns, confesses:

"Ottoman Muslims never neglect bathing and cleaning themselves. Even when they are ill and out of energy, they do so with the help of their servants, children or wives. When they die, their corpses are not placed in the coffin and given a ritual prayer before they are washed according to the rites of Islam. Yet, Europeans generally lose their sense of hygiene once they grow old and frail. And when they die and are to be placed in coffins, they are wrapped in the worst shroud they can find in the house. Even the thought of giving the corpse a quick scrub down never crossed anyone's mind."

Solomon Schweigger, a Protestant priest, also cannot help but praise Muslims:

"They cover themselves even when bathing. What manners! It seems that in spite of our dislike for them, we must learn some manners from these people!"

ENVIRONMENTAL CLEANING

Since man is a social being, he has to live together with other people. This brings along various rights and responsibilities towards them.

As he/she pays attention to the purity of his/her soul and body, a Muslim also pays utmost attention to the cleanliness of his house, street and surroundings. Because environmental cleanliness is an issue that concerns not only ourselves but also others. Polluting the environment means disturbing and harming other people. However, a Muslim is someone who does not harm others and does not hurt any living thing.

Keeping our environment clean is very important both for our own health and for the health of others.

A Muslim's house and other places should be neat and orderly, as if the Messenger of Allah – upon him blessings and peace - would come to visit him in the evening or in the morning.

By commanding us: "Clean your courtyards", Allah Messenger – upon him blessings and peace - stated that the surroundings of our houses should also be cleaned.

The Prophet – upon him blessings and peace - said:

"Beware of being of those who have been cursed."

Thereupon, the Companions – May Allah be well-pleased with them - asked:

"Who are they? O Messenger of Allah?" our Prophet responded:

"They are the ones who pollute the way people come and go and the places where they are shaded."

It is incompatible with Islamic ethics to disturb others by polluting the roads where people come and go, the places where they sit and rest.

When it comes to the masjid or mosque, shoes and slippers should not be left around, but rather they should be placed in a suitable place so as not to be an obstacle on people's way and disturb anyone.

Muslims houses should always be kept extremely clean. They take off their shoes at the door and never go inside with their shoes on. Everywhere in their houses is enough to perform prayer.

Our Prophet was the cleanest of people in terms of environmental cleanliness as well as body and clothing. As much as he cared about his own cleanliness and elegance, he wanted others to look clean, elegant and beautiful.

The Prophet was also very sensitive to environmental cleanliness. One day, he was going to attend an invitation with his companions. While walking on the road, he removed from the road the objects such as stones, trees, thorns that could trip people's feet and harm them and threw them aside. At the same time, he continued to chat with his companions. (Muslim, Iman, 58) At the time, the Prophet saw a man passing by, spitting on the street. This image seemed very ugly to him. His facial expression changed. He did not like this at all.

Our Prophet – upon him blessings and peace - wanted to clean this saliva himself so that other people would not be disturbed. However, his companions, who loved the Messenger of Allah very much and followed him carefully, understood that he was troubled and saddened by this. One of them immediately acted and covered this spittle by covering with dust.

When this unpleasant situation was resolved, the Prophet began to smile again and said:

"A Muslim should not harm his environment with his actions. As much as giving importance to the cleanliness of the body and the environment, he should also pay attention to the cleanliness of his inner world, that is, of his heart. When a servant commits a sinful deed, a black spot appears on his heart. If he does not repent and continues to commit this sin, the number of black dots increases and cover his whole heart. As if that person's heart gets rusted.

While a man was walking along the road, a thorny branch, or bush, came across in front of him. He did not want another passer-by to get entangled in the bush and get hurt, so he picked it up and threw it aside. Allah, the Exalted, was very pleased with his behavior and forgave his past sins. (Bukhari, Mazalim, 28; Muslim, Birr, 128) In this respect, removing sharp things that can harm people, or things like garbage that would disturb the eyes and hearts of people of the way, is a charity that Allah will reward. (Bukhari, Jihad, 72; Muslim, Musafirin, 84)

MOSQUE MANNERS

Thinking that the mosque is the house of Allah, it is necessary to show it utmost respect, to tidy it up when entering, and not to show a reckless attitude. The Messenger of Allah – upon him blessings and peace - explained this issue with the following hadith:

"When one of you enters the mosque, he should perform a two-cycle prayer of salutation before sitting down." (Bukhari, Salat, 60)

It is very important that the mosques are cleansed from all kinds of filth and behavior that people detest and hate.

According to a narration reported from Anas bin Malik, the Messenger of Allah saw a spit in the direction of the qibla of the mosque. He cleaned it with his own hand. The intensity of his anger at this was visible on his blessed face. (Muslim, Masajid, 52; al-Bayhaqi, al-Sunan al-Kubra, I, 255) The Prophet – upon him blessings and peace - wanted his ummah to be clean, gentle and elegant, and he wanted them to stay away from behaviors that contradict this.

The Messenger of Allah – upon him blessings and peace - said in another hadith:

"The deeds of my people, good and bad, were presented before me, and I found the removal of something objectionable from the road among their good deeds, and the sputum mucus left unburied in the mosque among their evil deeds." (Muslim, Masajid, 58)[1]

In this hadith, the issue of spitting in the mosque is dealt with. Mosques are places worship and places where Muslims congregate. It is necessary to pay maximum attention to the cleanliness of these holy places.

Essentially, cleanliness, which must be observed by every human being, has been transformed into a form of worship by Islam.

Our Prophet – upon him blessings and peace - did not want unpleasant odors on his clothes, especially when he was going to mosque. As a matter of fact, he took off a cardigan he was wearing when he sweated and felt the smell of wool. Aisha – May Allah pleased with her - reported that our Prophet always liked fragrances. (Abu Dawud, Libas, 19)

"Whoever eats something from this smelly vegetable, do not approach our mosque. Because angels are disturbed by what people are disturbed by."

What is meant by the smelly vegetable in the hadith is onion and garlic. Everything that smells has the

1. In those days, there were no carpets, rugs and similar covers in the mosques, and instead the floor was covered with sand. For this reason, spits could be seen around the mosque from time to time.

same ruling. What is meant by the angels' disturbance is that they dislike and hate such situations. Because they love good manners, cleanliness, beautiful and pleasant things; they are disgusted by the opposite of them.

In addition, our Prophet – upon him blessings and peace - said, "When you see someone shopping in the mosque, say, 'May Allah not make your trade profitable!'" and thus forbade Muslims from trading in the mosque. (al-Tirmidhi, Buyu', 76; al-Darimi, Salat, 118; al-Bayhaqi, 2/447)

The Messenger of Allah – upon him blessings and peace - said:

"When any one of you enters the mosque, he should say: '*Allahumma iftah li abwaba rahmatik* (O Allah! open for me the doors of Thy mercy)'; and when he steps out he should say: "*Allahumme inni as'aluka min fadlik* (O Allah! I beg of You Thy Grace)"! (Muslim, Musafirin, 68)

Reading

There was an old lady named Umm Mihjan who lived in one of the suburbs of the beautiful city of Medina. One day, this woman, whose thoughts and heart were as pure as she was, said:

"Since the Almighty Allah has cleansed my heart of unbelief and sin, and given me the purity of faith, then I should clean His house. Thus she started to clean the Prophet's Mosque every day."

Umm Mihjan's cleaning of the mosque was very pleasing to the Messenger of Allah. Our Prophet loved Umm Mihjan very much and every time he saw her in the mosque, he would smile and inquire about her health and wellbeing.

One day, Umm Mihjan, who was already old lady, fell ill. For days, she could neither clean the Prophet's mosque nor see his blessed face. Ummi Mihjan was so upset about this situation that she wanted to get well soon and continue her work in the mosque again. However her illness prevented her from going to the mosque. She was always crying out of her sadness.

When the Prophet – upon him blessings and peace - could not see her for a few days, he asked her neighbors. they said:

"She is sick, O Messenger of Allah!"

Upon this answer, the Prophet started walking towards Umm Mihjan's house, who lived in the sub-urbs of Medina. Some went to Umm Mihjan before the Prophet and said:

They said, "Good news to you, Umm Mihjan, our Prophet is coming to visit you."

When Umm Mihjan received this good news, she did not know what to do with excitement. Her heart, which had been weak due to her illness, began to beat rapidly. Before long, a sweet voice was heard:

"Assalamu Alaykum", it was the voice of our Prophet – upon him blessings and peace…

Umm Mihjan tried to get up and replied in a weak voice:

"Wa Alaykum al-Salam, O Messenger of Allah."

The visit was short, but it was very valuable for Umm Mihjan. Because the Prophet of Allah – upon him blessings and peace - had come to her visit. She would not be upset even if she could not get up anymore.

After that day, our beloved Prophet – upon him blessings and peace - often asked her neighbors how Umm Mihjan was. He received frequent information about the condition of her health. He advised her neighbors:

– If Umm Mihjan dies, do not bury her without my knowledge.

Finally, one evening, Umm Mihjan gave her pure soul to Allah. Her neighbors immediately washed her and enshrouded her. When the preparations were completed, they decided to go to the Prophet's house and ask him to lead the funeral prayer. However, the night prayer had been performed and it was quite late, and the Prophet – upon him blessings and peace – was resting in his house.

Those who were present at the funeral began to talk among themselves:

- What a good woman she was.

– She was cleaning the mosque whenever we saw her.

– Should we wake up our Prophet?

– It would not be appropriate for us to disturb the Prophet.

– However, our Prophet commanded us to inform him. Let us not make a mistake without knowing it!

– I think we should not disturb our Prophet!

Such hesitant conversations continued. In the end, Umm Mihjan was taken to the cemetery without informing the Prophet. The funeral prayer was performed and she was buried. When the Prophet – upon him blessings and peace - asked about her in the morning, his companions said,

- O Messenger of Allah! She passed away, we buried him. In fact, we came to you after we washed and shrouded her. But you were at rest. We did not want to disturb you."

Our Prophet was very upset. Because he wanted to lead her funeral prayer himself.

"Then come with me," he said, and went to the cemetery with his companions. Their neighbors showed Umm Mihjan's grave. The Prophet and his companions reperformed the funeral prayer for Umm Mihjan. They invoked Allah for her soul and left.

Our Prophet valued this woman with good character after her death as well as before her death, and showed a good example of loyalty to her. Thus, Umm Mihjan received the reward of her love for the Messenger of Allah and cleaning the house of Allah, both during her life and after her death. (It has been storified from Bukhari, Janaiz, 67.)

MANNERS OF VISITING PATIENTS

"The one who visits the sick is in fact like one who is in the fruit garden of Paradise so long as he does not return." (Muslim, Birr, 39)

Health and illness are two important reasons for which people are tested and warned against. With the feelings of praise and gratitude to Allah by not being heedless in healthy times, we should try to come closer to our Almighty Lord wholeheartedly with supplications and invocations in times of illness. Intelligent believers who make good use of both situations always profit in the end.

There are various diseases that people of almost all ages are suffered from. Illness is a source of sadness and distress. In cases of illness, a person wants to see his wife, friends and relatives next to him and to find solace with their sweet words and help. He even expects the people whom he did not get in touch throughout his life to visit him and ask how he is. He gets upset if they do not come his visit. For this reason, our beloved Prophet – upon him blessings and peace - ordered his followers to perform acts of social worship, such as visiting the sick, that brings people closer to each other. Bara bin Azib -May Allah be well-pleased with both of them- says:

"The Messenger of Allah – upon him blessings and peace - ordered us to do seven things and forbade us to do other seven. He ordered us: to follow the funeral procession. to visit the sick, to accept invitations, to help the oppressed, to fulfill the oaths, to return the greeting and to reply to the sneezer: (saying, "yarhamukallah (May Allah be merciful on you)," provided the sneezer says, "Alhamdulillah (All the praises are for Allah)". He forbade us to use silver utensils and dishes and to wear golden rings, silk (clothes), Dibaj (pure silk cloth)". (al-Bukhari, Janaiz, 2; Muslim, Libas, 3)

The sick person's state becomes heartbroken and sensitive. Almighty Allah is closer to the people with broken hearts. Since Allah Almighty likes His servants to visit the sick, He considers these visits to be made for Him. The Messenger of Allah – upon him blessings and peace - expresses this truth as follows:

"Verily, Allah, the Exalted and Glorious, would say on the Day of Resurrection:

"O son of Adam, I was sick but you did not visit Me." Son of Adam would say:

"O my Lord; how could I visit You whereas You are the Lord of the worlds?" Thereupon He would say:

"Did not you know that such and such servant of Mine was sick but you did not visit him and were you

not aware of this that if you had visited him, you would have found Me by him?" He would say

"O son of Adam, I asked food from you but you did not feed Me." Son of Adam would say:

"My Lord, how could I feed You whereas You are the Lord of the worlds?" He would say:

"Did not you know that such and such servant of Mine asked food from you but you did not feed him, and were you not aware that if you had fed him you would have found him by My side?" (The Lord would again say:)

"O son of Adam, I asked drink from you but you did not provide Me." Son of Adam would say:

"My Lord, how could I provide You whereas You are the Lord of the worlds?" Thereupon He would say:

"Such and such of servant of Mine asked you for a drink but you did not provide him, and had you provided him drink you would have found him near Me" (Muslim, Birr, 43)

Therefore, the servant should not think about whom he is visiting, but whose command he is carrying out. For this reason, the Prophet – upon him blessings and peace - advised his Companions to ask for an invocation from the sick person whom they visited and stated that the patient's invocation was like the prayer of the angels. (Ibn Majah, Janaiz, 1)

Visiting the sick means asking about the patient's condition and well-being, fixing his broken heart and meeting his needs as much as one can. In this context, visiting a patient is a muakkad sunnah of the Prophet. There are also scholars who think that it is a compulsory duty upon Muslim society. If no one visits a patient and does not meet his needs, all Muslims living there become responsible. Thus, just like feeding the hungry, visiting the sick becomes communal obligation (fard kifa-i).

Ibn Umar - May Allah be well-pleased with both of them - narrates the following incident about our Prophet's visit to the sick:

"While we were sitting with the Messenger of Allah – upon him blessings and peace -, a person, one of the Ansar, came to him and greeted him. The Ansari then turned back. Upon this the Messenger of Allah said:

"O brother of Ansar, how is my brother Sa'd ibn 'Ubada?" The man said:

"He is better." The Messenger of Allah said:

"Who amongst you would come to visit him with me?" He (the Holy Prophet) stood up and we also got up along with him, and we were more than ten persons. We had neither shoes with us, nor socks, nor caps, nor shirts. We walked on the barren land till we came to him. The people around him kept away till

the Messenger of Allah and his Companions with him came near Sa'd b. 'Ubada." (Muslim, Janaiz, 13)

In like manner, our mother Aisha - May Allah be well-pleased with her - describes this beautiful characteristic of the Messenger of Allah with the following striking example:

"Sa'd bin Mu'adh was wounded in the arm vein during the Battle of the Trench. The Messenger of Allah – upon him blessings and peace - had a tent set up for him in the mosque. His purpose was to visit (take care of) him more often and closely." (al-Bukhari, Maghazi, 30)

As it is seen, the Messenger of Allah – upon him blessings and peace - was closely interested in all kinds of problems of people. Behaviors based on love and compassion, such as inquiring about the sick, visiting his friends, trying to meet the needs of those in need, attending the funerals of the deceased and leading their prayers, and expressing condolences to those left behind, were manifestations of his good character. While performing social duties such as visiting the sick, he would often go with some of his companions and educate them in such matters. Being in poverty and need was not an obstacle to these visits. On the contrary, it enabled them to get closer to each other, to meet their needs jointly, and to share the blessings they had.

Regarding the visit of the sick, one should make no discrimination between Muslims and non-Muslims, acquaintances, close neighbors and distant neighbors. As a matter of fact, the Messenger of Allah visited a Jewish child who was sick and it was an occasion for the sick child to become a Muslim. (Bukhari, Janaiz, 80)

MANNERS OF OFFERING CONDOLENCES AND PARTICIPATION TO THE FUNERAL

"Muslims who suffer any calamity should think about the calamity that befell them after my death and find solace and be patient." (Muwatta', Janaiz, 41)

Offering condolences (*ta'ziyah*), which contains the meanings of comforting the person who is faced with a calamity and encouraging patience, generally refers to a visit made to express condolences and wishes to get well soon to the relatives of deceased. It is necessary to advise someone who has suffered a calamity to be patient, to be told that destiny is manifested in the disaster that has befallen, that it is no longer possible to reverse it, and that surrendering to destiny will bring one spiritual comfort. In addition, it is one of the most important manners of delivering condolences is to to remind that Allah Almighty gives rewards to the troubles that befall him, and to pray Allah for him/her with invocations such as "May Allah increase your reward", "May He grant you patience", "May He grant you gratitude". Because of such characteristics, offering condolences has the effect of reducing pain.

Offering condolences can be delivered by visiting personally or, if this is not possible, by other means of communication such as telephone and letter.

It is necessary to support spiritually a person who has suffered a hardship or who has lost a loved one, by offering condolences verbally as it is necessary to help him/her actually when necessary. As a matter of fact, when the news of the martyrdom of Ja'far al-Tayyar -May Allah be well-pleased with him- came to our Prophet – upon him blessings and peace -, he said *"Cook for Ja'far's family! Because they cannot be busy with the preparing food in this situation!"* (Abu Dawud, Janaiz, 25-26)

Offering condolences to a believer is one of the moral values of Islam. However, it is considered reproachable to offer condolences after three days in order not to renew the grief of the deceased. However, people far away who could not be present at the burial of the diseased can offer condolences after three days.

Examples from the Practice of the Prophet:

Zainab -May Allah be well-pleased with her- sent (a messenger) to the Prophet requesting him to come as her child was dying (or was gasping), but the Prophet returned the messenger and told him to convey his greeting to her and say:

"Whatever Allah takes is for Him and whatever He gives, is for Him, and everything with Him has a limited fixed term (in this world) and so she should

be patient and hope for Allah's reward." (al-Bukhari, Janaiz, 33)

The Messenger of Allah – upon him blessings and peace - stated that condolence is an important human duty and said: *"There is no believer who consoles for his brother for a calamity, but Allah will clothe him with garments of honor (grants honor) on the Day of Resurrection."* (Ibn Majah, Janaiz, 56)

The following letter, written by our Prophet to Muadh ibn Jabal -May Allah be well-pleased with him-, who was outside of Medina, on account of offering condolences the death of his son, is an example of such delicacy and condolence:

"Bismillahirrahmanirrahim.

From Muhammad, the Messenger of Allah, to Muadh ibn Jabal...

May the peace of Allah be upon you!

I would like to convey to you that I praise Allah, there is no god but He. Now; May Allah increase your reward and give you great rewards in return and give you the strength to be patient. May He bless us and you. For, our lives, our possessions, our good children, the sweet gifts of Allah, the Mighty and the Exalted, are among the things entrusted to us for a temporary period of time.

Allah made you happy by giving you that child. Now He has taken him from you for a great reward. If you expect mercy, forgiveness and guidance from Allah in return, be patient! Then you will regret it! Know that crying and whining cannot bring anything back, nor can it drive away sadness and grief. What is to come has already come, wa's-salam." (Hakim, III, 307)

Awf ibn Malik -May Allah be well-pleased with him- states the following in a narration stating that the Prophet – upon him blessings and peace - attended the funerals and prayed for them:

"Our Prophet led a funeral prayer. At the time, I heard the Messenger of Allah pray as follows and I memorized it:

"O Allah! forgive him, have mercy upon him, give him peace and absolve him. Receive him with honour and make his grave spacious; wash him with water, snow and hail. Cleanse him from faults as Thou wouldst cleanse a white garment from impurity. Requite him with an abode more excellent than his abode, with a family better than his family, and with a mate better than his mate. Admit him to the Garden, and protect him from the torment of the grave and the torment of the Fire."

When I heard this beautiful prayer, I thought to myself, "I wish I were that dead body." (Muslim, Janaiz, 85)

The Messenger of Allah – upon him blessings and peace - described the reward of performing the funeral prayer and sending the deceased to the grave as follows:

"(A believer) who accompanies the funeral procession of a Muslim out of sincere faith and hoping to attain Allah's reward and remains with it till the funeral prayer is offered and the burial ceremonies are over, he will return with a reward of two Qirats. Each Qirat is like the size of the (Mount) Uhud. He who offers the funeral prayer only and returns before the burial, will return with the reward of one Qirat only." (al-Bukhari, Iman 35)

ETIQUETTE FOR EXCHANGING GREETINGS

When a Muslim sees a Muslim brother or sister, he/she becomes happy.

Muslims love each other very much. When they come together, out of affection for seeing the people they love most, they become happy and exchange greetings with smiling faces. The love, happiness, and peace that believers feel in their hearts for each other are manifestations, or reflections, of Allah's attribute of "Salam" (Peace).

For this reason, when Muslims meet each other, they greet each other by saying "***As-salamu 'alaykum***" or "***Salamun 'alaykum***" ("Peace be upon you"). Those who are greeted respond by saying "***Wa 'alaykum as-salam***" or "***'alaykum as-salam***" ("And upon you be peace."). One meaning of Allah's name of "Salam" (Peace) is "***that which protects His servants from all kinds of evil, hardships, and afflictions and brings them to safety.***" From this perspective, giving and receiving *salams* has such nice meanings as "***O my brother, I am Muslim. No harm will come to you from me, be safe and secure*" and "*Our Lord's at-***

tribute of Salam surrounds us all, so live in peace and security."

Allah Almighty tells us of the importance of giving *salams* in the Qur'an:

"When a (courteous) greeting is offered you, meet it with a greeting still more courteous, or (at least) of equal courtesy. ..." (al- Nisa, 4: 86). What we can understand from this verse is that returning a *salam* to the person who gives it is commanded by Allah, a *fard* (obligatory act). As for the initial *salam*, it is a very important *sunnah* of our Prophet –upon him blessings and peace-.

What should we pay attention to while giving salam?

Allah the Exalted says:

"When a (courteous) greeting is offered you, meet it with a greeting still more courteous, or (at least) of equal courtesy ..." (al-Nisa, 4: 86)

When someone says ***"As-Salamu 'alaykum"*** we can return it by saying ***"Wa 'alaykum as-salam wa rahmatullah"*** extending it in a beautiful way.

To the person who greets by saying ***"As-salamu 'alaykum wa rahmatullah"*** (May the peace and mercy of Allah be upon you), there is also a beautiful way to extend our reply: **"Wa 'alaykumu's-salamu wa rahmatullahi wa barakatuhu"** (May the peace, mercy, and blessings of Allah be upon you). We receive an additional reward for each extension.

Our Prophet –upon him blessings and peace- would usually be the first one to say *salam*. We should also try to be the first to say *salam* when we meet someone.

When we come across an acquaintance or a friend, after saying *salam* we shake hands.

It is not necessary that we know a person for us to say *salam* to him or her; we also say *salam* to people we do not know.

Just as we say *salam* when we enter a gathering, we also say *salam* when we leave.

When someone says *salam* to us, we respond immediately with a voice loud enough for him/her to hear, not in a voice too quiet or too loud.

In saying *salam* or returning *salam*, we should not use a voice that is impolite and harsh or an intrusive and idle manner.

If we as a group enter a gathering or a crowded place, it is enough if one of us from our group says *salam*. If just one person from the crowd returns the *salam*, that is enough as well.

In exchanging greetings, the young should be the one to say *salam* to the old; likewise, same rule applies to someone from a small group to those in a larger group, someone walking to someone sitting, and someone riding to someone walking.

THE PLEASURE OF EXCHANGING SALAMS

Abdullah ibn 'Umar -May Allah be well-pleased with them-, would regularly go to the bazaar with Tufayl ibn Ubay -May Allah be well-pleased with him-.

One day, when Abdullah was walking to the bazaar together with his friend Tufayl, he saw a man selling old worn-out stuff and said *salam* to him. After that, he saw a merchant selling valuable goods and he said *salam* to him. Later, they saw a poor, forlorn man and Abdullah -May Allah be well-pleased with him- exchanged *salams* with him too. Then a rich man came and Abdullah -May Allah be well-pleased with him- also said *salam* to him. He said *salam* to many people, friends and strangers.

The next day Tufayl -May Allah be well-pleased with him- came again to his friend Abdullah ibn 'Umar -May Allah be well-pleased with them-. Abdullah said:

— Come on Tufayl, let us go to the bazaar! Be an accompany to me.

— What are you going to do at the market? You do not buy anything. You pass by so many shops and sellers and you do not even ask about the prices of their wares.

— Come on, let us go again.

— But if you are not going to buy anything why do you want to go to the bazaar? You do not sit and talk with people anyway. Let us stay here and talk.

— O Abu Batin ("Father of a pot-belly"),

Tufayl -May Allah be well-pleased with him- was a little overweight. When Abdullah got angry at his dear friend, or when he wanted to tease him, he called him Abu Batin.

— Look Tufayl -May Allah be well-pleased with him-, the only reason we are going to the bazaar is to say *salam*. We are saying *salam* to the people whom we meet there. (Malik, Muwatta', Salam 6), because our Prophet –upon him blessings and peace- said,

"You shall not enter Paradise so long as you do not affirm belief (in all those things which are the articles of faith) and you will not believe as long as you do not love one another. Should I not direct you to a thing which, if you do, will foster love amongst you: (i.e.) give currency to (the practice of paying salutation to one another by saying) as-salamu alaikum." (Muslim, Iman, 93)

In what situations do not we give or return salams?

In the toilet, bathroom or bath we do not give or return the *salam*.

We do not say salam to someone who is trying to lead one to sin or to someone who is committing a sin. If they say salam, we do not return it.

We do not say salam to someone who is performing ritual prayer or reading the Qur'an.

We do not say salam to someone who is reading a hadith, preaching, or reciting the call to prayer.

ETIQUETTE FOR SLEEPING AND RESTING

Allah Almighty has made the day bright for working and earning a living; and He has made the night dark for resting and sleeping. All creatures have been created with the need for resting and sleeping. While performing acts of worship or working, we must be relaxed, peaceful, and strong. Moreover, we need proper rest and sleep in order to be healthy.

What should we pay attention to when sleeping and waking?

We should go to bed early, in a state of ablution, after performing salat al-'isha'.

We should brush our teeth before sleeping.

We should sleep in clean sleeping clothes, pajamas.

We should recite Ayat al-Kursi, chapter al-Ikhlas, chapter al-Falaq and chapter an-Nas in bed before sleeping.

If possible, we should sleep by turning our face to the direction of qiblah and by placing our right hand under our chins.

In order not to place pressure on our heart, which is on the left of the body, and on our stomach, we should sleep on our right sides.

Because our Prophet –upon him blessings and peace- forbade it, we never sleep lying face down, on our backs with our legs crossed.

We should sleep neither too little nor too much. (6-8 hours)

We should not sleep while the sun is rising or setting. (within 45 minutes after sunrise and within 45 minutes before sunset)

We should sleep with the intention to wake up for dawn prayer or mid-night prayer so that our sleep will be spiritually rewarded as an act of worship.

Before sleeping, we should read the following supplications, which our Prophet –upon him blessings and peace- taught us.

اَللّٰهُمَّ بِاسْمِكَ اَمُوتُ وَاَحْيَا

"O Allah! I die (sleep) and come to life (wake) in Your name."

After waking, we praise our Lord and rise from our right side. Then we read this supplication.

اَلْحَمْدُ لِلّٰهِ الَّذِى اَحْيَانَا بَعْدَ مَا اَمَاتَنَا وَاِلَيْهِ النُّشُورُ

"Praise be to Allah who brings us to life after we die. The Resurrection will be to Him." (al-Bukhari, Da'awat, 8)

Our beloved Prophet –upon him blessings and peace- said to one of his companions:

— O so-and-so, whenever you go to your bed (for sleeping) say,

اَللّٰهُمَّ اَسْلَمْتُ نَفْسِى اِلَيْكَ وَفَوَّضْتُ اَمْرِى اِلَيْكَ وَوَجَّهْتُ وَجْهِى اِلَيْكَ. وَاَلْجَأْتُ ظَهْرِى اِلَيْكَ رَغْبَةً وَرَهْبَةً اِلَيْكَ لاَ مَلْجَأَ وَلاَ مَنْجَا مِنْكَ اِلاَّ اِلَيْكَ. آمَنْتُ بِكِتَابِكَ الَّذِى اَنْزَلْتَ وَنَبِيِّكَ الَّذِى اَرْسَلْتَ

'O Allah! I have surrendered myself over to you and have turned my face towards You, and leave all my affairs to You and depend on You and put my trust in You expecting Your reward and fearing Your punishment. There is neither fleeing from You nor refuge but with You. I believe in the Book (Qur'an) which You have revealed and in Your Prophet (Muhammad) whom You have sent.'

If you then die on that night, then you will die as a Muslim, and if you wake alive in the morning then you will receive the reward" (al-Bukhari, Da'awat, 7)

ETIQUETTE FOR EATING AND DRINKING

Allah Almighty says: *"...enjoy (all) things good and pure, and work righteousness: for I am well-acquainted with (all) that you do."* (al-Mu'minun, 23: 51)

Our Lord sent us to this world in order for us to become His excellent servants and go to Paradise.

In order to carry out the tasks prescribed upon us such as the acts of worship in a good manner, He has made halal (lawful) for us to meet our need such as sleeping, eating, and taking shelter. He bestowed upon us with countless blessings such as vegetables, fruits, meat, and milk. In turn, if we eat or drink of these bounties with the intention of becoming better servants of our Lord, the Creator of all the worlds, our eating and drinking will be a part of our worship. For instance, if a student eats with the intention to be strong enough to gain beneficial knowledge, Allah Almighty will immediately start rewarding his endeavor of learning. If a young eats dinner with the intention to wake up and perform dawn prayer and all his daily acts of worship for his Lord, then he will also start to be rewarded for all those acts of worship.

What should we pay attention to before starting to eat?

We must not eat until we feel hungry.

We should help prepare the table.

We should wait for our elders and visitors, if there is any, to sit first.

We should wash our hands before coming to the table.

We should use a tablecloth so no food pieces or crumbs fall on us.

If we eat sitting on the ground, we should sit on our left foot, with our right knee raised up. We should not lean on anything.

When eating at the table, we should neither lean back too far, nor lean over the table.

We should eat of our food with intention of using the energy it gives us to be good servants of our Lord and worship him well.

When we begin eating, we say "**Bismillahi'r-Rahmani'r-Rahim**" ("In the name of Allah, the Compassionate, the Merciful"). If we forget to say the basmala at the beginning of the meal, we should say "**Bismillahi awwalahu wa akhirahu**" (In the name of Allah, in its beginning and its end") as soon as we remember.

What should we pay attention while eating?

We should start eating our meal by eating some salt at the beginning and finish the meal again by eating some salt. This is a nice tradition of our Prophet –upon him blessings and peace-.

We should eat from what is in front of us with our right hand.

We should chew well every bite before swallowing it, and we should not take another bite before swallowing the first one.

We should close our mouths while eating so that we will not disgust anyone.

We should not find fault with any dish. Because the Messenger of Allah would not dislike any food, nor would he find fault with it. If he liked it, he would eat it, if he did not, he would leave it.

We should eat the food from what is in front of us, but while eating fruits, we can eat from wherever we like.

We should never do the following while eating and drinking!

We should not eat or drink anything prohibited by Islam.

We should not eat or drink while standing.

We should not drink water in one gulp. We drink it in three breaths and by taking a short rest between breaths. We should not breathe into the container.

When sneezing, coughing, or belching, we should not put food into our mouths; and we should close our mouths. Otherwise we will face a dangerous or disgusting situation.

We should not leave the top of water and food containers open. Because insects, flies and vermin can fall into it.

We should not eat or drink from plates or cups with broken rim. Because our lips and tongue can be cut.

While eating, we should not talk nonsense, we should not laugh and make noise.

We talk when we swallow our bite, not when we have food in our mouth.

We should not wipe our hands and mouths with a piece of bread and then swallow that piece of bread.

We should not throw the fallen bite in the trash just because it has become dirty. We wipe it, clean it and then eat it.

We should not blow on food that is hot; and we should not drink very cold water all at once.

We should not leave our food or plate unfinished. We should not spill crumbs.

What to do after eating!

When we finish eating, we should say, "al-hamdu li'llah" and "O Allah, thank You for this food." In this way we express our thanks to Allah and say the invocation for food.

After eating, we wash our hands.

When we eat together, we only get up together after everyone has eaten.

We should help to clear the table.

We should thank those who made the food and set the table.

Once when eating with his Companions, our Beloved Prophet –upon him blessings and peace- said the following:

— *"A human being fills no worse vessel than his stomach. It is sufficient for a human being to eat a few mouthfuls to keep his spine straight. But if he must (fill it), then one third of food, one third for drink and one third for air."* (al-Tirmidhi, Zuhd 47; Ibn Majah, At'ima 50)

Once a Companion forgot to mention Allah's name (*basmalah*) while eating until there remained the last morsel. When he raised it to his mouth, he said: In the name of Allah at the beginning and at the end of it (Bismillahi awwalahu ve akhirahu). The Prophet smiled -upon him peace and blessings- and said:

"The devil kept eating along with him, but when he mentioned Allah's name, he vomited what was in his belly." (Abu Dawud, At'ima 16)

Later, to promote blessings while eating, he said,

— *"The food of one is sufficient for two, and the food of two is sufficient for four, and the food of four is sufficient for eight."* (Muslim, Ashriba 179; Tirmidhi, At'ima 21)

A DATE-TASTED MEMORY

My name is Rafi bin Amr. Let me tell you about a memory that I had with the Messenger of Allah in my childhood and that affected me deeply.

I was only six or seven years old. I was playing on the street, I did not notice how the time passed. It was such a day again. I got hungry. As usual, I was too lazy to go home. I decided to go to the nearest date orchard and steal dates from there. I sneaked into the garden and began to stone the palm trees. I was throwing stones, soil, twigs, whatever I could find on the ground to the date tree and trying to drop dates. After a while, maybe ten times more dates than I would eat some ripe, some unripe were fallen on the ground. I had eaten a few of the ripe ones from the bunch, filling my stomach well, when the owner of the orchard saw me. He grabbed me by the arm and took me straight to the Messenger of Allah – upon him peace and blessing be -. The owner of the orchard said:

— O Messenger of Allah, here is the boy who stoned my palm trees! This boy is harming my date palm trees. I have been on the lookout for him for a long time.

He put me in front of the Messenger of Allah. He wanted me to be punished. I was little, I could not make much sense of what was going on; but I was very scared. The Messenger of Allah smiled at me and stroked my hair saying:

— "O little one! Why do you stone the date palms?" I responded innocently,

— "Sir. I got hungry while I was playing and wanted to feed myself." That Prophet of mercy smiled at my answer, given from an innocent child and patted me on the back. Then he said,

— "O my son! The next time you get hungry, eat of the dates that have fallen to the ground. They are both softer and sweeter. In this way, you will not harm the trees or the dates of the owner of the orchard." Then, he said,

— "O Allah! Fill this child's belly with halal food," and prayed Allah for me.

While I was afraid of what would happen next, I never forgot the Messenger of Allah stroking my back with a smile and giving me gentle advice. Since that day, I have never harmed anyone else's property. I did not take anyone's belongings without permission. I paid great attention to the fact that everything I ate and drank was halal. These beautiful moments with the Prophet -upon him peace and blessings- deepened my view of life and the world. In my later years, I understood better how important halal and haram and the right of the slave are. I have never touched haram. (Based on the hadith of Ibn Majah, Tijara, 67.)

ETIQUETTE FOR YAWNING, SNEEZING, COUGHING, AND BELCHING

All of us yawn, sneeze, couch and belch because these are natural human actions. However, when we do, we should not bother or disturb the people around us. Imagine you are excitedly explaining what you think to a friend and he begins to yawn. Imagine someone comes up to you and coughs or sneezes in your face. How would you feel? Or if someone who had eaten garlic or onion burped in your ear, what would you think? Of course, these are very inappropriate actions that we should never do, right?

A good Muslim is always a kind, polite and agreeable person. A Muslim does not bother anyone with his actions or the states he finds himself in, and he does not gross anyone out. He always treats those around him with pleasantness and beauty.

What should we pay attention to when yawning or coughing?

Because yawning is due to drowsiness, absent-mindedness, heedlessness, or similar reasons, we should try to control ourselves when yawning if it is possible.

When we have to yawn, we cover our mouth with our hands and try to shorten the yawning time.

We should take care not to make too much noise when we yawn.

Since cough is mostly caused by respiratory tract diseases, micro-organisms and bacteria inside the mouth are thrown out during coughing. To prevent this, we cover our mouths with a handkerchief or, if there is no handkerchief, with our hands.

While coughing, to prevent spittle from shooting out of our mouths, and to keep from making a lot of noise, we should close our mouths.

While coughing, we should turn slightly to the left and downwards. If at this time we are either talking or listening to someone, we should apologize by saying "Excuse me."

What should we pay attention to while sneezing and belching?

Sneezing is the relief of pressurized air from inside us, thrown out quickly. It is something that is good for our bodies' health, so every time we sneeze we say, **"Al-Hamdulillah"** ("Praise be to Allah").

When we hear someone sneezing, we should say, **"Yarhamukallah"** ("May Allah have mercy on you").

After sneezing and saying **"Al-Hamdulillah,"** if someone responds to us saying **"Yarhamukallah,"** then we should reply to them saying **"Yahdina wa yahdikumullah"** ("May Allah guide us and you").

While other statements may be said in place of the above-mentioned ones, the best ones are those that our Prophet taught us.

Most of the time, when it comes to us not being able to stop ourselves from belching, it is for reasons such as eating too much, too fast, drinking soda, and eating food such as onions and garlic that produce gas. We should take measures against this.

When we eat, we should chew each bite well and swallow slowly so air does not enter our stomachs and cause us to belch.

We should refrain from eating too much.

When we are going to go to the mosque or attend a gathering, we should not eat foods like onion and garlic that causes gas and belching and emits unpleasant smells.

Even though we try not to, if we cannot help belching, we should do it silently and cover our mouths with our hands.

If possible, we should go somewhere with no one around to belch.

We should always keep in mind the following saying of our beloved Prophet –upon him blessings and peace-, **"A Muslim is a person who never harms anyone with his hand or his tongue,"** and never disgust or disturb anyone.

UPTO THREE TIMES

While the Messenger of Allah – upon him blessings and peace - was talking with his Companions, one of them sneezed quietly. Thereupon, our Prophet –upon him blessings and peace- said, "Yarhamukallah." A short time later, another companion sneezed. However, the Messenger of Allah –upon him blessings and peace- did not say anything.

The one to whom our Prophet –upon him blessings and peace- did not say "Yarhamukallah" then said, feeling slightly offended:

– O Messenger of Allah! Someone sneezed and you said "Yarhamukallah." I also sneezed, but you didn't make such an invocation for me. After he said this, our Prophet –upon him blessings and peace- said:

– Upon sneezing, that man said "al-Hamdulillah," but as for you, you did not say it. (al-Bukhari, Adab, 127)

He –upon him blessings and peace- then said:

— When you sneeze, say "Al-Hamdulillah" ("Praise be to Allah"). Then your brother or friend should respond by saying "Yarhamukallah" ("Allah have mercy on you"). Then the person who sneezed should say, "Yahdikumullah wa yuslihu balakum"

("May Allah guide you and rectify your state.") (al-Bukhari, Adab, 126) and further added,

— If someone sneezes more than three times, it is enough that his brother say "Yarhamukallah" three times because that means he has a cold. (Abu Dawud, Adab, 92)

MANNERS OF BROTHERHOOD

People who lived in tribes before Islam were constantly at war. Wars waged out of little pretexts were fought for the honor of the tribe. The bond of kinship preceded the bond of religion and belief. After the advent of Islam, religious brotherhood took precedence over everything else. In line with the Divine command **"The Believers are but a single Brotherhood: So make peace and reconciliation between your two (contending) brothers; and fear Allah, that you may receive Mercy."** (al-Hujurat, 49: 10) the Blessed Prophet –upon him blessings and peace- declared a brotherhood amongst the believers. After that, the feeling of religious brotherhood took precedence over kinship bonds. So much so that in the Battle of Badr, which was the first battle of the Muslims, some Muslims fought with their brothers, some with their fathers, and some with their uncles. As a matter of fact, on that day, Abu Bakr –May Allah be well-pleased with him- came face to face with his son; and Abu Ubayda ibn Jarrah –May Allah be well-pleased with him- against his father; and Hamza –May Allah be well-pleased with him- against his own brother.

After the Migration to Medina, the Ansar from Medina became such brothers with the Muhajirs from Mecca that they made them partners in their own house. They gave half of their garden and fields. They showed an unprecedented example of sacrifice and generosity.

Our brother deserves the best of our service and care

The Blessed Prophet –upon him blessings and peace- offered the following advice to a group of Companions, just before they set out to visit another group of brethren:

"You are coming to your brethren; so tidy your mounts and tidy your dress, until you are like a mole among the people. Allah does not like obscene words or deeds, or do intentional committing of obscenity." (Abu Dawud, Libas, 70)

Brothers are responsible towards one another! Brothers have rights over each other!

A brother runs to his brother's help, sees to his need; for whosoever takes care of a brother's need in this life will have Allah, glory unto Him, take care of his need in the Hereafter. (Bukhari, Mazalim, 3)

A brother does not expose the faults of his fellow brother. Whosoever conceals the deficiencies of a brother in this life, Allah, glory unto Him, will conceal his faults in the Hereafter. (Muslim, Birr, 58)

Muslims seek to patch up relations, not destroy them. They do not backbite and spread gossip.

Believers visit each other only for the sake of Allah, glory unto Him, in good times and bad.

Muslim brothers always nurture well-wishes for each other.

They express their love for another.

If a believer must tell another of his mistake, he talks to his brother with the best of intentions and in private. He acts like a mirror that reflects to him what he is.

A brother also loves and respects his brother's loved ones.

Brothers never hate or do not envy or hold grudges against each other. Thus they do not stay offended for more than three days.

Brothers do not look down on each other.

A brother prays for his fellow brothers who have become entrapped in the swamp of sin. He tries to save them and give them a helping hand out of their situation.

In showing mutual mercy and compassion towards one another, Muslims are like the organs of a single body. When one of the organs hurt, it distresses the rest of the body. For instance, during a toothache, we instantly raise our hand to our cheek for comfort.

Our feet carry the whole body to the dentist, just to have the aching tooth treated. The eyes share its pain by losing sleep and staying awake. The entire body mobilizes itself to heal the pain of a single tooth. And likewise, no matter how geographically distant they may be from each other, all Muslims are like the organs of a single body.

Hasan Basri –may Allah have mercy on him- once had a man come to him and say,

"I went to so-and-so's house the other day and he said malicious things about you."

"Why did you go to his house to begin with?" asked Hasan Basri.

"I was invited there for a meal", he replied.

"Well, what did he serve you?"

"Many things…Soup, roast meat, sweets, milk…"

In response, Hasan Basri said:

"You were able to keep all those things you ate in your stomach and you could not keep a couple of words to yourself?"

A LEGENDARY FEAT (A STORY)

The Battle of Yarmuk was a fierce battle that tested the patience of all Companions. There were only 46,000 of them, facing a daunting Byzantine army of 240,000 men. Muslim soldiers whose hearts filled with the love of Allah and His Messenger, fought gallantly. Under the command of Khalid ibn Walid, praised by the Blessed Prophet –upon him blessings and peace- himself, they gained a blitzing victory. They had given 3000 martyrs and slain around a 100,000 Byzantines. The victory was indeed a legendary feat of bravery and sacrifice almost unequalled in history.

The battle was drawing to an end. The entire battlefield, scorched all day by the blistering sun, was covered by hurling dust. Having now fought for hours on end, the brave Muslims were carrying spear, arrow and sword wounds. They had not found even a moment's opportunity to drink the sun-warmed water out of their water bottles. Lips craving for a drop of water were, one by one, sipping the potion of martyrdom that would cool them down for eternity, mumbling the word of tawhid with their parched tongues. Huzayfa –May Allah be well-pleased with him- recounts these scenes of sacrifice made by men giving up their loves for the sake of Allah, glory unto Him, and the eternal happiness of humankind:

"I was wounded and exhausted. With what remained of my strength, I got up on my feet and went looking for my cousin Harith. I was moving amid my brothers, laying across the field, living their final moments in life, moaning from the pain of their mortal wounds. Before long, I found him. He was carrying multiple wounds. I kneeled towards him, with my water bottle in hand.

He had no energy left to speak. However, he was trying to tell me something with his eyes. When I hurriedly opened the lid of the bottle and held it out to him, to unite his cracked lips with the water he had been longing for, I heard the voice of brother Iqrimah, lying wounded on the ground close to where we were.

'Water! Water! Please...a drop of water" he was moaning. It turns out that on hearing the voice of Iqrimah, my cousin was signaling me, with his eyes, to take the water bottle to him instead.

I immediately ran towards Iqrimah, who had let go of his body, pierced by from multiple sword and spear wounds, on the scorching sand. I held out my bottle to his mouth. He seized it and lunged forward to take his first drink. That was when we heard the moans of our brother Ilyas, from not so far away.

A drop of water, please...For the love of Allah!' he was groaning.

Before the warm water could even touch his lips, Iqrimah handed the bottle back to me; and slowly turned his head towards the direction of Ilyas, signaling me to take the bottle to him. He could not bear to have even a drop of water his brother Ilyas was agonizingly moaning for.

When I ran to Ilyas, I found him drawing his last breath, saying the word of tawhid. His Lord had taken Ilyas to His eternal mercy, allowing him to gulp the springs of Paradise before he could ever lay his parched lips on the water Iqrimah had foregone for him. Instantly, I ran back to Iqrimah, thinking that I should at least deliver the water to him. But by the time I arrived next to him, he too had long drunken the beverages of Paradise offered to martyrs. Harith was still alive, at least; so I ran this time to him. But like the others, Harith stood in no need of water anymore.

THE MANNERS OF GIVING-RECEIVING GIFTS

Exchanging gifts strengthens the bonds of love.

Gifts are what we offer to our loved ones without expecting anything in return. Presenting gifts help destroy selfishness, miserliness and ill-feelings of jealousy. Receiving gifts, in turn, amplify feelings of mercy and compassion, like a pinch of sugar dropped in the glass of water. It erases any prior hatred and hardheartedness between the giver and the receiver.

The Blessed Prophet –upon him blessings and peace- informs how offering gifts helps bring believers together and strengthens their bonds of love:

"Offer gifts to one another; for a gift wipes out malice and hatred from the heart. Let not any woman belittle any gift she offers her female neighbor, even if it be a little piece of mutton." (al-Tirmidhi, Wala, 6)

"Offer a gift back to him who offers a gift to you. If you are not able to find anything, then at least pray for him so that the gift is not left unreturned." (al-Nasai)

What to pay attention when offering gifts?

Gifts should be offered and received with the intention of fulfilling a sunnah of the Blessed Prophet –upon him blessings and peace, and a deed of worship.

One should not take note of the material value, quality or the size of a gift. What is important in offering or receiving gifts is the value two people mutually place upon one another and their mutual love.

When offering a gift, if the desire to show off or an expectation of a favor in return finds its way into the heart, the gift will lose all its value. The gift will not produce feelings of love, compassion and brotherhood.

The gift must not be out of one's budget; for remembering and being remembered is what is important, not the material value of the gift.

If possible, we should buy or prepare the gift with our own means.

Those who deserve our gifts the most are our family members, our relatives, friends and neighbors but most of all, our dearest mothers, who have done far more for us than anyone.

We should wrap our gift in the best way possible and offer it with a smile and polite, gentle words.

It also a sunnah of the Blessed Prophet –upon him blessings and peace- to present personal items to people who happen to like it.

"A woman once brought a mantle she had knitted with her own hands to the Messenger of Allah –upon him blessings and peace- as gift. She said:

'I knitted this with my own hands so that you could wear it, Messenger of Allah.'

Needing a mantle of the kind, the Messenger of Allah kindly accepted the gift, wore it and then came next to us. Someone who saw him remarked, 'What a beautiful mantle… Can I have it?'

'Sure', replied the Messenger of Allah –upon him blessings and peace-. After sitting awhile, he then returned home; and after nicely folding the mantle, sent it to the man as gift." (al-Bukhari, Libas, 18)

What kind of gifts are unacceptable?

Things considered unlawful or vile by Islam cannot be offered or accepted as gift.

Things that will scare or upset a person cannot be given as gift.

If the gift is offered as bribe or as reason to cause injustice, which are prohibited by Islam, then the gift cannot be accepted.

A SINGLE SHIRT

The Blessed Prophet –upon him blessings and peace- would love giving away the things that he owned as gift. If a person wanted something from him, he felt obliged to give it. There were times when he would give away the very last food or the sole item of clothing he had.

In fact, one day a child came to him and said, "My mother wants a shirt from you."

The Blessed Prophet –upon him blessings and peace- had only the shirt he was wearing at the time and nothing else to wear.

"I will give you a shirt…but come a little while later", he said to the child.

The child went back and returned not long afterwards.

"My mum urgently needs any shirt you can give her", he said. Thereupon the Blessed Prophet –upon him blessings and peace- went inside his room. He removed the shirt he was wearing and handed it to the child. The Companions, who arrived at the Masjid a short time later, found out that the Blessed Prophet –upon him blessings and peace- had given away the only shirt he had and therefore was unable to come to Masjid for prayer. They immediately obtained a shirt and gave it to the Messenger of Allah –upon him blessings and peace-.

With his unique and unmatchable generosity, the Blessed Prophet –upon him blessings and peace- was a superb example to entire humankind.

SHOWING RESPECT TO THE ELDERS

Man is an honored and dignified being.

Due to their longer life, elders possess a greater knowledge and experience compared to children and the young. In a family, elders like grandfathers, grandmothers, uncles, aunts are people who have contributed to our growth and development. They merit greater honor and respect than anyone. Therefore, in the Islamic culture, the young always respect their elders, give them priority, and consider serving them a duty. The elders, too, treat the young with love, compassion, and understanding. In this way, a bond of love and respect emerges between the young and the old. This creates a peaceful environment in Muslim society.

How do we show respect to our elders?

In a seated environment, on seeing an elder walk inside, we stand up and if needed, show him a place where he can sit; and wait for him to do so.

If the elder is someone of old age or vast knowledge, we show him respect by kissing his hand.

We know that the priority of speech always belongs to our elders. We either talk when they have finished talking or we ask permission to talk.

Ibn Umar –May Allah be well-pleased with him-recounts:

I was still a small child when the Messenger of Allah –upon him blessings and peace- asked a group of elders around him to name a tree that resembles the features of a Muslim; the tree which always bears fruits and is evergreen."

Nobody there spoke to name the tree that the Messenger of Allah –upon him blessings and peace- was thinking of. I thought in my mind that 'this must be the date tree'; but because I was next to the Companions like Abu Bakr and Umar –Allah be well-pleased with them-, I thought it would be inappropriate to state my opinion. Moments later, the Messenger of Allah –upon him blessings and peace- confirmed what had been crossing my mind. 'It is a date tree', he said.

Then when I left the gathering along with my father, I told my father that the name of the tree had occurred to me when the Messenger of Allah –upon him blessings and peace- asked the question.

'Then why did you not say it?' my father asked. 'It would have made me so happy to see you give the right answer!'

'Seeing all of you keep silent', I answered, 'I thought it would be more appropriate for me to keep my silence, too (when in fact I could have spoken when none of them could think of the answer)'. (See, Bukhari, Ilm, 4 Adab, 79)

We do not raise our voice when speaking to our elders. We keep our wits about us and do not act in a shameless manner.

We do not act rudely by making gestures with our hands and arms.

When eating with elders, we wait for them to start first.

When walking with them on the street, we do not walk in front of them. Rather, slightly behind them and to their left.

If we see them carrying a heavy bag in their hands, we carry it for them.

We run to their help wherever they may be and for whatever help they may need.

On vehicles of public transportation, we vacate our seats for them, should they be unable to find an empty seat.

When they leave from a gathering, we stand up and see them to the door.

One day the Blessed Prophet –upon him blessings and peace- was sitting with his Companions. Right next to him were Abu Bakr and Umar –Allah be well-pleased with them-. Then suddenly, Abbas –May

Allah be well-pleased with him-, the Prophet's –upon him blessings and peace- uncle, turned up. Abu Bakr made up room for Abbas; and Abbas sat right between the Prophet and Abu Bakr. The Blessed Prophet –upon him blessings and peace- then said:

"Only the courteous and refined know the value of courteous and elegant people."

While talking with his uncle, the Blessed Prophet –upon him blessings and peace- had lowered his voice so much that Abu Bakr said to Umar:

"Something has happened to the Messenger of Allah…it seems that he has lost his voice; and that has me worried". Abbas eventually left moments later, whereupon Abu Bakr asked the Blessed Prophet –upon him blessings and peace-:

"Were you not feeling well before, O Messenger of Allah?"

"No", replied the Prophet –upon him blessings and peace-.

"It made me worried to hear you lowered your voice so much…" Then the Blessed Prophet –upon him blessings and peace- explained:

"Just as Angel Gabriel has advised you to lower your voices next to me, he has advised me to lower my voice next to my uncle." (Ali al-Muttaqi, Kanz al-Ummal, V. XIII, 514/37321)

THIS IS HOW RESPECT IS SHOWN!

The Blessed Prophet –upon him blessings and peace- would listen to everyone out until they finish talking. He would never interrupt anyone's talk. To those who extended their hands to him to shake, he would offer his hand and would not draw it back until the other person drew his hand back. Throughout the duration of their chat, the Blessed Prophet –upon him blessings and peace- would listen by looking directly at their faces and would not turn his gaze elsewhere until the person had done so. (al-Tirmidhi, Qiyamah, 46)

The Blessed Prophet –upon him blessings and peace- was always happy to see youngsters respectfully helping their elders. he would say *"Allah the Almighty blesses a young person who shows respect to an elder because of his age, with people to serve him in his old age"*. (al-Tirmidhi, Birr, 75)

One day the Companions Abdullah and Muhayyisa went to the town of Khaybar. They were going to meet a friend there. When their friend failed to show up at the agreed spot, they became worried and went out in search of him. Soon afterwards, they found him lying dead in a ditch, covered in blood. Terribly upset, they returned to Medina. When Abdurrahman, Abdullah's brother, was informed of what had happened, he took Muhayyisa as well as his brother Huwayyisa to the Blessed Prophet –upon him blessings and peace-. There, the young Abdurrahman excitedly began explaining the incident, at the top of his voice, letting no one else speak; when in fact Muhayyisa, who was not only personally part of the incident and but also older than him, was right by his side.

Not pleased with Abdurrahman's attitude, the Blessed Prophet –upon him blessings and peace- cautioned him with the following words, *"Leave the speech to your elders...leave the speech to your elders."* (al-Bukhari, Jizya, 12) Thereupon, Abdurrahman went quiet and left the explaining to his elders.

The Blessed Prophet –upon him blessings and peace- was fond of talking with a medium tone and piecemeal, word by word. He never talked in a high pitch, as addressing a deaf person or in an argument. He used to set the best example in polite and courteous speech, both to his own grandchildren and other children. He would advise them to speak in a soft tone, when talking to both their seniors and juniors. As an example, he would quote the advice that Luqman –upon him peace- gave to his son: **"And be moderate in your pace, and lower your voice; for the harshest of sounds without doubt is the braying of the ass."** (Luqman, 31; 19)

The Blessed Prophet –upon him blessings and peace- desired all people to show mutual respect. Just as he wished for juniors to respect their elders, he also wished for elders to value and love their juniors. He would say, *"He who does not love and value his juniors and does not honor and respect his elders is not from us."* (Tirmidhi, Birr, 15)

IF ONLY THEY TOOK A LESSON (A STORY)

Murad II, the great Ottoman sultan, recalls one of his memories:

We had crushed the Crusaders on the battlefield of Varna. In the aftermath, I wandered around the field, observantly inspecting the slain soldiers of the crusading army. One thing I noticed was that they were mostly young.

Turning to Azap Bey, the experienced commander of countless battles

I remarked, 'Almost not a single old man amid this massive pile of bodies, Azap…Not a single man with grey in his hair…What do you say?

Azap Bey understood the subtle point I was trying to make and smiled. After a moment's silence, he said,

They would not have dared to face a strong and courageous army and steer themselves into disaster, if they had enough old men to speak sense into them…

Perhaps all their elders already took the lesson that your late grandfather Bayazid had given them on the battlefield… More than enough fear to hold them back! (referring to the victory at Nigbolu forty-eight years ago)

MANNERS OF LEARNING

The Prophet – upon him blessings and peace - said: *"Either be a teacher, a learner, a listener, or a lover of knowledge. Do not be the fifth (beyond these) and you will perish."* (Majma al-Zawaid, vol.1, p.122.)

Ali -May Allah be well-pleased with- said: "I will be the slave of anyone who teaches me a letter," and thus pointed out the importance of learning and respecting the teacher.

For all competent believing men and women, it is individual obligation (fard 'ayn) to acquire knowledge about acts of worship such as wudu, ghusl, prayer, fasting, zakat and pilgrimage together with the knowledge about Islamic creed.

Acquiring knowledge sometimes becomes a communal obligation (fard kifa-i). It is a communal obligation to learn the sciences necessary for the operation of worldly affairs, such as medicine, calculus, syntax, grammar, reading and writing, and learning the chains of the narrators of the hadiths.

Sometimes learning can be haram. As a matter of fact, it is haram to learn sciences such as sorcery, magic, and divination.

The following hadith of the Messenger of Allah – upon him blessings and peace - is sufficient to express the value of knowledge: *"If anyone travels on a road in search of knowledge, Allah will cause him to travel on one of the roads of Paradise. The angels will lower their wings in their great pleasure with one who seeks knowledge, the inhabitants of the heavens and the Earth and the fish in the deep waters will ask forgiveness for the learned man. The superiority of the learned man over the devout is like that of the moon, on the night when it is full, over the rest of the stars. The learned are the heirs of the Prophets, and the Prophets leave neither dinar nor dirham, leaving only knowledge, and he who takes it takes an abundant portion."* (Abu Dawud 3641; al-Tirmidhi 2682; Ibn Majah 223).

"Wisdom and knowledge are the lost property of the believer. Wherever he finds it, he will take it." (al-Tirmidhi, 'Ilm, 19)

".. And when you are told to rise up, rise up Allah will rise up, to (suitable) ranks (and degrees), those of you who believe and who have been granted knowledge..." (al-Mujadila, 11)

The following are the points that one should pay attention to in the journey of knowledge, which is such an important job:

Patience:

The traveler of knowledge must be patient and compete in patience. If jihad is patience for an hour, then seeking knowledge is patience for the rest of our lives.

Being sincere in deeds:

It is the most important thing not to depart from sincerity in the deed. Our aim should be reaching the pleasure of Allah and the Hereafter, we should avoid hypocrisy/show off, and stay away from the desire to be arrogant towards our friends. The Messenger of Allah – upon him blessings and peace - said: *"Whoever learns knowledge in order to argue with the dissolute, to show superiority to scholars, or to attract people's attention to himself, his place will be in Hell."* (al-Nasai 2654)

To act according to the knowledge:

Acting with knowledge is the fruit of knowledge. Whoever learns and does not act according to his knowledge will be like the Jews whom Allah denounced: **"The similitude of those who were charged with the (obligations of the) Mosaic Law, but who subsequently failed in those (obligations), is that of a donkey which carries huge tomes (but understands them not). Evil is the similitude of people who falsify the Signs of Allah: and Allah guides not people who do wrong."** (al-Jum'a, 62: 5)

Study the books:

After memorizing and consolidating the summaries, it is necessary to study, take notes and spare time for the books that cover the topics comprehensively. Recording details, problem solutions, and ambiguous differences of rulings helps one to acquire depth on a subject. One should never be content with a piece of information heard, on the contrary, try to memorize and interpret it.

The books that are needed should be read as much as possible, because such books are a means of education, but by increasing to study them, knowledge increases. We should make use of such books as much as we can.

To be determined:

Perseverance has a very high share in learning. It is an important motto not to settle for less if possible to collect more. It is necessary to learn useful topics without delay. Hope and procrastination can deprive the traveler of knowledge from that knowledge. There are many downsides to procrastination. It is a common saying that "*halaka'l-musawwifun*: those who postpone are destroyed".

Making good use of time:

The seeker of knowledge should appreciate the times when he is vigorous and free, healthy, young and when he is less busy. It is necessary to spend the time in the right places before obstacles such as family, children, income etc. arise.

Being polite towards the teacher:

In principle, knowledge is not taken from the book, on the contrary, a teacher is required to get the keys of knowledge in order not to make mistakes. Therefore, one should not fail to show respect to the teacher. Because this is the key to success.

It is necessary to treat the teacher with respect and courtesy at all times. It is necessary to be equipped with respect and decency while sitting, speaking, asking questions and listening...

Even when turning the pages of the book, one should behave in a manner of decency. It is necessary to abandon talking before the teacher and talking at length.

Also, it is necessary not to interfere with the teacher's speech. It is more appropriate not to ask private questions, especially in front of other people.

The student should not give boredom to his teacher. Calling him only by his name is a good deed, but it is appropriate to call him my teacher or our teacher.

If teacher makes a mistake, it should not discredit him from your eyes, as this deprives you of his knowledge. Who can be free of mistakes?

THE MANNERS OF ENTERING AND LEAVING THE HOUSE

Homes are places in which everyone lives in peace and comfort. Better or worse, our homes are the places in which we feel most comfortable. People are free at home; they eat, drink, walk around, rest and sleep however they please. At times, they also have their private moments which they do not want anyone else to see. There are therefore some rules that we must pay attention to when entering or leaving a house, be it our own, our friend's or someone else's

Allah the Exalted says:

"If you find no one in the house, enter not until permission is given to you: if you are asked to go back, go back: that makes for greater purity for yourselves: and Allah knows well all that you do." (al-Nur, 24: 28)

"O you who believe! enter not houses other than your own, until you have asked permission and saluted those in them: that is best for you, in order that you may heed (what is seemly)." (al-Nur, 24: 27)

Our beloved Prophet – upon him peace and blessings - said:

"Asking permission is thrice: If given permission you enter; if not, you turn back." (al-Bukhari, Istidhan, 13)

What to pay attention to when entering or leaving a house?

When entering a house, we need to knock on the door and ask permission, even if the house be our own.

When about to enter someone else's house, we do not knock on the door more than three times.

While waiting for permission to enter at the front of the door, we turn slightly to the side, so that once the door opens, we do not immediately see who/what is inside.

On being asked 'Who is it?', we respond by clearly stating our names and, if need be, our surnames.

If the door is already open, we still say '*assalamu alaykum*' or ask permission to enter before stepping inside.

Whether it be our own home or somebody else's, we should enter a house cheerfully and have nice things to say.

When leaving, we bid farewell to those who we leave behind, extending our best wishes and wishing upon them the protection of Allah, glory unto Him.

YOU MUST ASK PERMISSION (STORY)

At the age of eight, his mother left Anas ibn Malik –May Allah be well-pleased with him- to the Blessed Prophet –upon him blessings and peace- so that her son could serve the Prophet –upon him blessings and peace. The little Anas served the Messenger of Allah –upon him blessings and peace- up until the age of twenty. Receiving the special training of the Prophet –upon him blessings and peace- until he was twenty, Anas went on to live another seventy years after the passing away of the Prophet –upon him blessings and peace-. He loved the Blessed Prophet –upon him blessings and peace- so much that he never kept him out of his mind. Anas –May Allah be well-pleased with him- would say:

"There has never been a night in which I have not seen the Messenger of Allah –upon him blessings and peace- in my dream. Inshallah, when I reunite with him in the Hereafter, I will say, 'Look, O Messenger of Allah…your little servant Anas has come' and ask for his intercession."

Anas –May Allah be well-pleased with him- passes on one of the fine wisdoms he learnt from the Blessed Prophet –upon him blessings and peace-:

"The Messenger of Allah said to me, 'Give your greetings to your family, my dear, when you enter home so that that your salam serves as blessings both for yourself and your family.' (al-Tirmidhi, Istidhan, 10)

Another man once came to the Messenger of Allah –upon him blessings and peace- and asked, 'Am I supposed to ask permission even from my mother when I am entering home?'

'Yes', replied the Messenger of Allah –upon him blessings and peace-.

'But I live with her', said the man.

'You must still ask her permission', said the Messenger of Allah –upon him blessings and peace-.

'But I am always in her service', added the man.

'You must still ask...Would you like to see her naked?' asked the Messenger of Allah –upon him blessings and peace-.

'No!'

'In that case ask permission before you enter.' (Muwatta, Istidhan, 1)

What not to do when entering or leaving a house?

One must never peep through the keyhole, the window or any other place before entering the house.

When at somebody else's house, we do not meddle with or go through anything without the permission of the homeowner.

We do not look inquisitively at the merchandise or furniture inside the home –as if looking to buy them-.

We do not try to catch sight of people in other rooms from where we are sitting.

We do not lend an ear to the conversations taking place in other rooms.

After knocking on the door and asking permission to enter, we do not barge through the front door before actually the permission is given.

In the case of an emergency which requires us to leave immediately, we inform the homeowner, even if it be with a note.

Sahl ibn Saad –May Allah be well-pleased with him- explains:

A man was trying to peer inside the Prophet's –upon him blessings and peace- through a hole on the door. At that moment, the Messenger of Allah –upon him blessings and peace- had a comb in his hand. Becoming aware of the unwelcome behavior of the man, he said, "If I knew you were spying on me with malicious intent, I would have pierced your eyes with this comb. Asking permission before entering a house has been commanded only to *ensure that the interior of the home is protected from sight.*" (Muslim, Adab, 40, 41)

MANNERS OF NEIGHBORHOOD

"My love for those who do not cut off their relations with relatives and friends and those who visit each other is justified." (Ibn Hanbal, V, 229)

Going to see someone, to ask how they are, to take their heart, is a necessity of being a Muslim and of Islamic brotherhood. Allah Almighty declared all Muslims as brothers and ordered them to love and respect each other and to help each other. One of the most important reasons that helps to establish love among people is to visit each other. In this respect, Islam has given great importance to visitation.

Visiting neighbors can be done on various occasions such as illness, holiday, birth, death. There are also visits made out of courtesy without any reason. Muslims find the opportunity to help each other by learning about each other's troubles, problems and needs through visits.

"He who fills his stomach while his neighbor is hungry is not a true believer." (Hakim, II, 15)

At the same time, they develop the feeling that they are not alone in the society, and they look to the future with hope and confidence. Their siblings, whom they see around them in moments of joy and sadness, become a source of peace for them. For this reason, there are many benefits to visit the neighbors and acquaintances. Based on such benefits, the Messenger of Allah used to constantly visit his Companions. Qays bin Sa'd -May Allah be well-pleased with- describes one of his visits as follows:

"The Messenger of Allah -upon him blessings and peace-came to visit us in our house, and said:

"Peace and Allah's mercy be upon you!" My father returned the greeting in a lower tone. I said:

"Do you not grant permission to the Messenger of Allah -upon him blessings and peace-to enter?" My father said:

"Leave him, he will give us many greetings." The Messenger of Allah -upon him blessings and peace-then said:

"Peace and Allah's mercy be upon you!" My father again responded in a lower tone. The Messenger of Allah -upon him blessings and peace-again said:

"Peace and Allah's mercy be upon you!" So the Messenger of Allah -upon him blessings and peace-went away.

My father went after him and said:

"O Messenger of Allah! I heard your greetings and responded in a lower tone so that you might give us many greetings." The Messenger of Allah -upon him blessings and peace-returned with him. My father then offered to prepare bath-water for him, and the Prophet took a bath. My father then gave him a long wrapper dyed with saffron or wars and the Prophet wrapped himself in it.

The Messenger of Allah -upon him blessings and peace-then raised his hands and said:

"O Allah, bestow Your blessings and mercy on the family of Sa'd ibn Ubadah!" The Messenger of Allah -upon him blessings and peace-then shared their meals.

When the Prophet intended to return, my father brought near him an ass which was covered with a blanket. The Messenger of Allah mounted it.

My father told me:

"O Qays, accompany the Messenger of Allah." The Messenger of Allah said to me:

"Ride." But I refused. He again said:

"Either ride or go back your home (do not get tired)." I said:

"So I went back." (Abu Dawud, Adab, 127-128)

In another hadith, it is reported that the Messenger of Allah visited a family of Ansar, ate food in their house, performed prayers and prayed Allah for them. (al-Bukhari, Adab, 65)

The Messenger of Allah used to order his ummah to visit their sick and brothers and sisters in religion. He said in a hadith:

"Whoever visits a sick person or a Muslim brother for the sake of Allah, a caller calls out to him: "What a beautiful and pleasant deed you have done. By doing this, the reward of your walk was also good, and you prepared a place for yourself in heaven!" (al-Tirmidhi, Birr, 64)

Visits should be made only for the sake of Allah, not for any benefit. Allah Almighty has stated that He loves those who visit with sincere intentions. The following is stated in a sacred hadith:

"My love has become a right for those who love each other for My sake, give a lot in charity for My sake, those who are sincere in loving each other, those who do not break their relations with relatives and friends, and those who visit each other." (Ibn Hanbal, V, 229)

Regarding the visit of the sick, one should make no discrimination between Muslims and non-Muslims, acquaintances, close neighbors and distant neighbors. As a matter of fact, the Messenger of Allah visited a Jewish child who was sick and it was an occasion for the sick child to become a Muslim. (al-Bukhari, Janaiz, 80)

"Serve Allah, and join not any partners with Him; and do good- to parents, kinsfolk, orphans, those in need, neighbors who are near, neighbors

who are strangers, the companion by your side, the wayfarer (ye meet), and what your right hands possess: For Allah loveth not the arrogant, the vainglorious." (al-Nisa, 4: 36)

MANNERS TO BE OBSERVED IN RELATIONSHIP WITH NON-MUSLIMS

Muslims should not greet non-Muslims when they meet them, and when the non-Muslims greet first, it is necessary for Muslims to reciprocate by saying "*wa alaykum*". The Messenger of Allah – upon him blessings and peace - said, *"Do not greet Jews and Christians first!"* (Muslim, Salam, 13) Again, the Companions of the Prophet asked to our Prophet:

"People of the Book greet us, how should we greet them?" Our Prophet said:

"Say wa alaykum." (Muslim, Salam, 7)

The following incident narrated by Aisha -May Allah be well-pleased with her-reveals the reason for this attitude that should be taken towards unbelievers. Aisha said: "A group of Jews entered the Messenger of Allah – upon him blessings and peace - and said, "As-Samu alaikum: Death be upon you!" I immediately noticed the sentence they said and told them, "as-Samu alaykum wa al-la'natu: Death and curse be upon you!" Allah's Messenger warned me by saying:

"Slow down, O Aisha! Allah likes to treat all matters with grace!" I said,

"O Messenger of Allah! Didn't you hear what they said?" Thereupon, the Messenger of Allah said:

"I already said them, 'Wa alaikum: On the contrary, it is on you!'"" (Bukhari, Adab, 35)

However, greetings can be given to a group of non-Muslims among whom there are some Muslims. For, our Master met a group of Muslims, polytheists and Jews and greeted them. (Bukhari, Isti'zan, 20)

THEY TOOK REFUGE IN US (A Story A Lesson)

During the time of Caliph Umar, a trade caravan came and stopped outside Medina for the night. They fell asleep immediately from exhaustion. Meanwhile, while everyone was sleeping, Caliph Umar was walking around the city. While he was walking around, the following incident happened.

Umar came to Abdurrahman bin Awf's house and lifted him from his bed and said:

"A caravan came tonight. All are infidels. But they took refuge in us. They are many and valuable. I'm afraid foreigners, passengers will rob them. Come, let's protect them. Abdurrahman ibn Awf replied:

"That would be great, you thought very well, I'll be right back."

They waited for the caravan in turns until morning. Then they went to the mosque for Dawn Prayer.

A young man in the caravan woke up at that time. He followed them and went after them. He investigated and learned that the person guarding them was Caliph Umar with his friend. He came and told this to his friends:

"O Friends! Do you know that two Muslims waited for us until the morning and prevented our belongings from being stolen?" The man's friends replied:

"Do you want us to believe that Muslims have no other business than to protect us? Moreover, they know that we are Christians." The man continued:

"And do you know who that man was?" They asked

"Who was he?"

"He was Umar, Caliph of Muslims." The men said,

"You have mistaken. What would the caliph be doing here at this time of night? He would probably be lying on a feather bed in his palace." The man said:

"Like you, at first I couldn't believe what I saw.

"Then how did you believe?"

"When it was morning and there was light, they left. Out of curiosity, I followed behind. They entered the mosque. I asked someone whom I met on the way "Who is this?", he replied "Our caliph Umar". The man continued:

"What are we waiting for?"

Listening carefully to what the man had said, the people of the caravan fell into a deep silence. There was no one left to talk or say anything. After a long silence, one of them broke the silence:

"What are we waiting for? Isn't this enough as a proof that Islam is the true religion?"

Others also agreed with this statement. Seeing the level of mercy and compassion of the great Caliph, who was famous for his justice and devastated the armies of Rome and Iran, they understood that Islam was the true religion, and they all willingly converted to Islam.

MANNERS OF HOSTING GUESTS AND VISITING OTHERS

According to our religion guests are treated like a trust coming from Allah. They are valued an esteemed. And we do everything to make them comfortable. We offer them our best food and host them in the nicest part of our houses. We treat them with utmost care, mercy, compassion, generosity, and sensitivity.

How do we host our guests?

We meet our guests at the door with a smiling face and say them “welcome“.

We offer them from the best part of our food and drinks.

We do not raise our voice and shout at someone from our family in front of our guests.

We do not secretly talk to one of our family members in front of our guests.

We do our best not to bore our guests by falling all over them.

By saying goodbye we see our guests off at the door of our house where we welcomed them when they first came to our house.

Our Prophet (peace be upon him) said that:

- When Allah wishes the goodness of one of His servants, He sends him a gift. This gift is a guest. The guest brings his blessings with him, but Allah forgives the sins of the household members because of the nice treatment and respect that they have shown to their guest. Anybody who believes in Allah and the Last Day should entertain his guest generously. (al-Bukhari)

To what do we pay attention when we go to visit someone?

We do not go to visit someone during the hours of the day reserved for sleeping, having meals, and resting (early in the morning, resting hours in the afternoon, and late at night).

We wear clean and nice clothes for our visit.

When we arrive at the door, we should knock it for once or twice; when we hear the voice saying "who is there?" we should respond by saying our name, e.g. "I am Ahmad" and enter the house and greet the household members after the landlord gives us his permission to enter.

We should meet our guests with a smiling face and talk to them nicely.

We should take a gift, even if it is something small, with us to the person we visit and should not go empty handed.

We should respectfully accept and eat and should not belittle the food and drink offered to us by the landlord.

We should not be curious about the things and people in the other rooms of the house and should not go and peek in them.

We should not stay long in the house we are visiting; we should not make visits too often to bore the landlord, because our beloved Prophet (peace be upon him) said to Abu Huraira who had too frequently visited him:

— O Aba Huraira! O Aba Huraira! Come every other day so that your love can be stronger.

If we visit the old and sick people, there is no problem if we increase the number of our visits to them.

We should say goodbye and thank to the host before we leave.

Jabir (May Allah be well-pleased with him) narrated one of his memories as follows:

I came to the Prophet in order to consult him regarding my father's debt. When I knocked on the door, he asked, "I"

- "Who is that?" I replied:

- He said, "I, I?"

- He repeated it as if he disliked it. (Bukhari, Istidhan, 17: Muslim, Adab, 39)

Luqman Hakim's beautiful advice to his son:

My Dear Son!

- Watch your heart during prayer in the presence of your Lord,
- Watch your tongue when you are with people,
- Watch your hand when you are eating,
- Watch your eye when you are visiting someone!

LET US PUT THE LAMP OFF

Our beloved Prophet (peace be upon him) was the most generous and self-sacrificing of all people. He would offer everything he had to other people and never become afraid of getting poor. Sometimes the Prophet – upon him blessings and peace - , however, could not find anything to give. In fact one night a man came and said to the Prophet:

— I am hungry.

Upon this, Allah's Messenger sent a message to his wife and asked her to prepare something to eat. It was however a time of famine and they had nothing at home left to eat. The respectful wife of Allah's Messenger sent a message back to the Prophet:

— I swear to Allah we have nothing left in our house other than some water.

Allah's Messenger – upon him blessings and peace - would never return anybody who was in hardship empty-handed. It was one of his best manners to offer the best of food to his guests and to share whatever he had with the people in need. This time however he had nothing to give. Our beloved Prophet turned to his companions with him:

— "who would like to take this man to his home as a guest?"

One of the Muslims of Medina said:

— "I can host him O Messenger of Allah!" and took the poor man to his home. When they arrived at home, he told to his wife meeting them at the door:

— "this man is going to be our guest tonight. Do we have anything at home to eat?" and his wife replied:

— "we have little food just enough for our children!"

The companion said:

— "Then keep the children a little bit busy. Let them sleep if they ask for supper. When our guest enters the room, I will find an excuse and put the lamp off. Then we will pretend to be eating. Our Lord asks us to spend and make sacrifices from the things that we hold dear. This is a test by which we can demonstrate how good believers we are, because Allah the Almighty knows our situation and is aware of every good deed we do.

Then companion's wife prepared the meal. The hospitable companion found an excuse, put the lamp off as he had agreed with his wife before, and the joined the dinner. They pretended to be eating with their guest in order to make the little amount of food satisfy his hunger. But the companion together with his wife and children went to deb hungry.

The next morning the companion bade farewell to his guest and went to the Prophet – upon him blessings and peace - . When the Prophet – upon him blessings and peace - saw the companion, he smiled and said:

— "Allah the Almighty became pleased and contented with the generosity and self-sacrifice that you demonstrated tonight!" (Bukhari, Manaqib al-Ansar, 10). (According to some reports this companion and his wife were Ali and his wife Fatima (May Allah be well-pleased with them.)

Then our Prophet – upon him blessings and peace - recited the following verse:

"And they give food out of love for Him to the poor and the orphan and the captive: We only feed you for Allah's sake; we desire from you neither

reward nor thanks. Surely we fear from our Lord a stern, distressful day. Therefore Allah win guard them from the evil of that day and cause them to meet with ease and happiness.” (al-Insan, 76: 8–11)

THE MANNERS OF TRAVELLING

Believer's travel is similar to merchant marketing merchandise. Just like a travelling salesperson commercializes his product to his clients in every place he goes, a believer always aims to earn spiritual rewards by doing good deeds and giving charity. His only object is and will always be to gain the pleasure of Allah the Almighty in every place he has been before and he travels in the future.

For example we, as Muslims, put our trust in Allah and pray Him during our journeys and thus earn spiritual rewards. We shorten our ritual prayers and benefit from the facilities which we are allowed to use during our journey, but we still earn spiritual rewards. We visit the tombs of Muslim scholars and the friends of Allah, contemplate about their good deeds, life and death, and thus earn spiritual rewards. If there is any scholar, or relatives, or friends living in the cities we stop by, we visit them for the sake of Allah and thus earn spiritual rewards. We observe and take lessons from the memories of the earlier nations that lived in the places we visit. We watch the scenery during our journey and think about greatness of the power and the art of our Lord and make spiritual profit.

The students who travel to learn Islam from the Muslim scholars collect rewards for every step they take and enrich their spiritual world. Even a tradesman who travels just to sell goods and make profit with the intention to spend part of his earnings for the sake of Allah will have done a praiseworthy deed.

To what we pay attention during our journeys?

Allah the Almighty says that:

"...Say: Travel in the earth and see how He makes the first creation, then Allah creates the latter creation; surely Allah has power over all things." (al-Ankabut, 29: 20)

"...Say: Travel in the land, then see what was the end of the rejecters." (al-An'am, 6: 11)

We travel with good intentions so that our journey turns into an act of worship.

If it is possible we set out for our journey on Thursday as our Prophet – upon him blessings and peace - used to do. Mondays and Saturdays can also be chosen.

Before we set out for a journey, we learn from the books of Islamic law how to perform our acts of worship (for instance ritual prayers, fasting, or wiping over the socks while performing ablution etc.) during a journey.

In order to get the most out of our journey and our time, we set out for a journey early in the morning, for our beloved Prophet – upon him blessings and peace - prayed saying that *"O Allah, bless my people in their early mornings!"* (Abu Dawud, Jihad, 78)

We do not go out for a journey alone and at night as much as possible. Instead we would prefer travelling with some company.

Upon our Prophet's advice, if we are travelling along with at least two other people, we choose one of us as our leader to obey his rules.

During long journeys, we choose the safest place if we need camping at night.

We do not make unnecessary stops and hang around.

Because our Prophet – upon him blessings and peace - counted "the invocation of a traveler" among the prayers which will not be refused by Allah the Almighty, we say as many prayers as possible for our family, relatives, friends, and for the entire nation of believers during our journey.

We stop and help those who are experiencing troubles and cannot continue their journey for some reason so that they can continue to travel.

If we have enough space in our vehicle, we offer a ride to our brothers and sisters in Islam whom we come across on our way and who do not have a vehicle.

If one of our travel mates gets sick or tired, we wait for him/her and help him/her to get the necessary medical attention.

We chat with our friends travelling with us whenever we get a chance. And we also help the elderly travelers when it is needed (such as to carry their luggage, and to hold their hands etc.)

We treat our travel mates with patience, compassion, and generosity. We do not tell them such things which may upset them. We especially stay away from actions which may lead to arguments.

We do not make bothersome noises and avoid disturbing behavior especially when we travel with a group of people.

In public transportation vehicles, we give our seat to senior citizens, the old, the sick, the pregnant women, and to those who are very tired in order to make them comfortable.

When we travel in public transportation vehicles, we do not eat or carry foods and drinks which may disturb others with their smell.

When we come back from our journey, we bring gifts to our family, friends, and to our respected teachers even if it is something small and cheap. Because this was our beloved Prophet – upon him blessings and peace - 's custom.

When returning from long journeys, we thank Allah the Almighty for bestowing us a healthy trip and allowing us come back to our home and family safe and sound by performing a two-cycle prayer of gratitude.

Our beloved Prophet – peace be upon him – used to recite the following verse from the Holy Qur'an when he was getting on his ride for the journey:

بِسْمِ اللّٰهِ مَجْرِيهَا وَمُرْسِيهَا اِنَّ رَبِّى لَغَفُورٌ رَحِيمٌ

"...in the Name of Allah will be its moving course and its resting (of this animal I am riding). Surely, my Lord is Oft-Forgiving, Most Merciful." (Hud, 11: 41)

After he settled on his ride, he would say "Allahu Akbar" three times and then recite the following verses:

سُبْحَانَ الَّذِى سَخَّرَ لَنَا هذَا وَمَا كُنَّا لَهُ مُقْرِنِينَ.
وَاِنَّا اِلَى رَبِّنَا لَمُنْقَلِبُونَ

"And Who has created all the pairs and has appointed for you ships and cattle on which you ride, that you may be seated on their backs and then remember your Lord's blessing when you are seated on them, and say, 'Glory be to Him, who

has subjected this to us, and we ourselves were not equal to it." (al-Zuhruf, 13: 12-13.)

AN EXEMPLARY JOURNEY

Full moon reflected on the desert sand and the night opened its gates to its sacred travelers with all its desolateness and tranquility. The companions were resting after a long and tiring journey under the burning desert sun. Then the caravan's watchman returned and brought back the Prophet's commands.

Our beloved Prophet – upon him blessings and peace - gave the following commands:

- Allow your camels and horses to graze when you travel through places with abundant grass,

- Ride your camels fast in order to keep their strength and to arrive the destination as soon as possible when you travel through arid and infertile places, (Muslim, Imarat, 178)

- When you intend to encamp at night, keep away from the road and set up your camp on the roadside,

- Unload your mounts and let them rest,

- Allah the Almighty loves leniency and understanding so treat your animals leniently.

That night the companions rested in accordance with the Prophet's orders. The following day they camped at some place on their way. They scattered and each one of them encamped in different glens and valleys. So the Messenger of Allah (peace be upon him) said:

"Your scattering in these glens and wadis is only of the devil." They afterwards kept close together when they encamped and never scattered. (Abu Dawud, Jihad, 97)

"In that journey our beloved Prophet waited until morning and then returned to Medina. As soon as he entered the city, the first thing he did was to go to the mosque and perform a two-cycle prayer. He thanked his Lord." (Bukhari, Maghazi, 79)

When he arrived his home, he had nice gifts in his bag for the members of his family. (Narrated based on the sayings of the Prophet –upon him blessings and peace-eported in the related sources.)

LOVING THE YOUNGSTERS

A flower flourishing in the wilderness gives us happiness. When we see a kitten or a puppy, we want to pet it. Everybody likes to see, smell, and caress a newborn baby, because Small things are lovable! They deserve to be treated with patience, understanding, and tolerance.

Our beloved Prophet (peace and blessings be upon him) loved the little children very much. Whenever he saw a child, his face would be covered with happiness and joy. When he saw a baby, he would embrace, caress, and kiss him/her. When he saw kids playing on the street, he would go to them, salute them and then join their play. Sometimes he would make jokes to them and sometimes he would give them presents.

How do we show our love to the children?

We always treat our children with compassion and mercy.

We take their mistakes kindly, and treat them with forgiveness.

We include them into our plays and entertainment as much as possible and join their plays.

We share our clothes and toys with them and give them gifts.

We kindly teach them the good and right manners by talking to them nicely. We become a role model for them to follow by our actions and behavior.

We encourage them to perform the acts of worship and perform our ritual prayers with them.

We assist them in their classes and other educational activities.

We immediately run for their help whenever they need.

Abdullah b. Abbas – May Allah be well-pleased with them - narrated:

— I was still a child. Whenever I saw Allah's Messenger perfoming prayer, I would go next to him and perform my prayer next to him, whereas I did not know how to perform prayer at the time. One night I stayed overnight in the house of my aunt Maimuna bint Al-Harith (the wife of the Prophet – upon him blessings and peace -). That night Allah's Messenger was staying there. We performed the night prayer together in congregation. Then the Prophet – upon him blessings and peace - slept for a while, and then got up at night. My aunt was also awake. They thought that I was sleeping, but I heard everything they talked. Allah's Messenger looked at me and said:

— "The boy had slept." I smiled and said:

— I am getting up. Then I got up and performed ablution just like they did. I stood up by his left side but he made me stand to his right. My aunt was praying behind us. We performed our prayer together. I would never forget that prayer and the excitement and joy I felt from it. (Bukhari, Ilm, 41)

I WAS SOLD CHEAP!

Mahmud b. Rabi met with the Messenger of Allah when he was a small child. Mahmud relates one of his memories as follows:

One day we were playing with our friends in the streets of Medina… Then we saw that the Prophet – upon him blessings and peace - was coming towards us…

We immediately made a circle around him. The Prophet of Mercy was happily looking at us with compassion and mercy. Encouraged by his endless tolerance, we said to him:

— O Messenger of Allah! We captured you. From now on you become our slave…

He became very happy and joined our play saying:

— Alas! You captured me as your slave, so what are you going to do to me now? When we said:

— We can let you free with only one condition. He asked:

— I will do whatever you want. Tell me what do I need to do? We said:

— We will let you go if you give us a ransom. He said:

— But I do not have much money on me. We them told him:

— Give us whatever you have. It is okay for us.

Allah's Messenger – upon him blessings and peace - sent Bilal (May Allah be well-pleased with him) to his home to bring some date fruits from his home. When we got the dates, we let the Messenger of Allah free. He smiled and left pretending to be sad saying:

— Just like my brother Joseph who had been sold for a trifle amount of money at the slave market, I was sold cheap.

THE MANNERS OF FRIDAY

Allah the Almighty loves His servants very much. He wants them to enter Paradise. This is why He bestows upon us from His endless treasures and offers us many opportunities. In order to forgive the people's knowingly or unknowingly committed mistakes and sins, He informs us about special days and nights. He also bestows great rewards for little deeds performed at such special times. Friday is one of those special times.

Allah's Messenger (peace and blessings be upon him) said:

"... The sun does not rise nor set, upon a day that is more virtuous than it. In it, there is an hour in which no believing worshipper makes a supplication to Allah for good, except that Allah answers it for him, and he does not seek Allah's aid for something, except that He aids him in it." (Tirmidhi, Tafsir, Buruj, (3336)).

One should start to get ready for Friday in the night before.

Our beloved Prophet (peace and blessings be upon him) would begin to get ready for Friday in the night before. He would take a nice bath lustration. In the

Friday morning he would put on his nicest clothes. He would wear some nice perfume and comb his hair. He would get a haircut and clip his finger nails if he needed. He would always remember Allah the Almighty with both his tongue and heart. Friday was special and valuable day for him. On his way to the mosque, every place that he passed by would smell like roses. He showed us how to spend Fridays through his personal application:

One should willingly go to Friday prayer and rush to go it.

Our Almighty Lord states in the Qur'an:

"O you who believe! When the call is made for prayer on Friday, then hasten to the remembrance of Allah and leave off trading; that is better for you, if you know." (al-Jumu'a, 62: 9)

Allah's Messenger (peace be upon him) informs us that whoever goes to Friday prayer earlier will get the most spiritual rewards:

"When it is Friday, the angels stand at every door of the mosque and record the people in the order of their arrival, and when the Imam sits (on the pulpit for delivering the sermon) they fold up their sheets (manuscripts of the Qur'an) and listen to the mention (of Allah). And he who comes early is like one who offers a she-camel as a sacrifice, the next like one who offers a cow, the next a ram, the next a hen, the next an egg." (Muslim, Jumu'a 24, (850)).

On Friday one should invoke blessings upon the Messenger of Allah as many times as possible.

Our Prophet (peace be upon him) informed:

— *Among the most excellent of your days is Friday; on it Adam was created, on it he died, on it the last trumpet will be blown, and on it the shout will be made, so invoke more blessings on me that day, for your blessings will be submitted to me.*

The people asked:

O Messenger of Allah! How can it be that our blessings will be submitted to you after you die and your body is decayed?

He replied: Allah, the Exalted, has prohibited the earth from consuming the bodies of Prophets."

— *If any one of you greets me, Allah returns my soul to me and I respond to the greeting."* (Abu Dawud, Salat, 201. Abu Dawud, Manasik, 96)

We should also excitedly and respectfully invoke blessings upon our beloved Prophet so that the Messenger of Allah (peace be upon him) personally responds to our prayers and invocations.

MANNERS OF SHOPPING

Human is a creature in need of eating-drinking, housing, etc. These needs vary according to the situation, position and level of the people. While meeting material needs, essential needs should be determined and care should be taken not to waste. The needs of the soul should not be regarded as essential needs.

"...Finally, on that day, you will certainly be brought to account for the blessings (that you benefit from in this world)." (al-Takasur, 102: 8)

The Messenger of Allah – upon him blessings and peace - expressed the recipe for happiness necessary to attain peace of mind as follows:

"Look at those who stand at a lower level than you but don't look at those who stand at a higher level than you, for that is better-suited that you do not disparage Allah's favors." (Muslim, Zuhd, 9)

"...Whoever looks to one above him for his religion, and follows him in it, and whoever looks to one who is below him in worldly matters, and praises Allah for the blessings He has favored the one who is above him with, then Allah writes him down as grateful and patient. And whoever looks to one who is below him

for his religion, and looks to one who is above him for worldly matters, and grieves over what missed him of it, Allah does not write him down as grateful nor as patient." (al-Tirmidhi, Qiyamah, 58)

Scarcity or abundance of goods is not important but the important matter is where we earn it and where we spend it.

The Messenger of Allah says:

"The feet of the son of Adam shall not move from before his Lord on the Day of Judgement, until he is asked about five things: About his life and what he did with it, about his youth and what he wore it out in, about his wealth and how he earned it, and spent it upon, and what he did with what he knew." (al-Tirmidhi, Qiyamah, 1)

One should not go for shopping just to spend time and have fun.

"(The believers) turn away from things that are vain and useless." (al-Mu'minun, 23: 3)

While shopping, Attention should be paid to waste.

Extravagance is an effort to buy reputation with property in order to suppress the feeling of inferiority. Allah Almighty explains what kind of a disaster it is as follows:

"Behold, the squanderers are, indeed, of the ilk of the satans..." (al-Isra, 17: 27)

In this regard, Allah Almighty has ordained that His servants should live with sensitive measures. In various verses, he specifically states the criteria that believers should observe in their spending and donations:

"(Those sincere servants of the Most Gracious) who, whenever they spend on others, are neither wasteful nor niggardly but [remember that] there is always a just mean between those [two extremes]." (Furqan, 25: 67)

Just as thirst cannot be quenched with sea water, it is not possible for man to satisfy his spiritual needs with mortal worldly possessions. Mortal things always increase suffering. In the end, a burning regret remains.

For this reason, the solution to waste, is to spend and give charity by living a contented, economical and simple life.

"(Those who have taqwa) who spend [in His way] in time of plenty and in time of hardship…" (Al Imran, 3: 134)

Attention should be paid to whether the products to be purchased are halal or haram.

Allah Almighty states the following in this regard in a verse:

“Eat of the things which Allah has provided for you, lawful and good; but fear Allah, in Whom you believe.” (al-Maida, 5: 88)

In many verses, substances that are haram to eat and drink are listed; It is ordered to stay away from eating unjustly the property of orphans, from interest, from gambling and from all kinds of unjust gains.

There is a beautiful story regarding the halal sensitivity of the Companions of the Cave told in the Qur’an:

The Companions of the Cave who chose to emigrate in an effort to preserve their faith and were put to sleep for 309 years in the cave where they took refuge, as a result of an extraordinary divine power and faith. When they wake up, they send one of them to the market and warn him saying:

“…Let, then, one of you go with these silver coins to the town, and let him find out what food is purest there, and bring you thereof [some] provisions...” (al-Kahf, 18: 19)

In this verse, the care that should be taken by people living in a land of disbelief and heedlessness regarding halal-haram has been expressed in the best way possible.

Halal leads the person to halal.

Ali Ramitani -may Allah sanctify his soul- said:

"A person who does not eat halal cannot find the strength to obey Allah and always tends to rebel His commands. A person who eats halal cannot be a rebel against Allah." In like manner, it is stated in a verse;

"Shun everything that is (materially - spiritually) dirty and unclean!" (al-Muddassir, 74: 5)

One should not shop from places involved with haram business activities

One should not shop at places that are not suitable for the Muslim identity such as places selling alcohol, trading with interest, etc.

Umar -May Allah be well-pleased with her- said, "Whoever puts himself in a position that may cause the believers' suspicion has no right to condemn those who blame him." (Kanz al-Ummal, hadith no. 8815)

One should pay attention to religious sensitivities

While going out for shopping, one should pay attention to the physical and moral requirements of Islamic dress code (hijab).

Attention should also be paid to the manner of speaking and tone of voice. (One should not speak in a way that attracts attention)

MANNERS OF TALKING AND LISTENING

The manner of speaking in Islam:

1. One should speak clearly and intelligibly according to the level of the addressee, and repeat the important points of the speech when necessary. As a matter of fact, the following points pointed out by the Companions about our Prophet, who spoke in a clear and eloquent style, are very important:

"The Messenger of Allah – upon him peace and blessings - spoke in a distinct manner so that anyone who listened to him could understand it." (Abu Dawud, Adab, 18)

"The Prophet – upon him peace and blessings - used to talk so clearly that if somebody wanted to count the number of his words." (al-Bukhari, Manaqib, 23)

"The Messenger of Allah – upon him peace and blessings - would repeat the words and phrases he wanted to be understood thoroughly three times." (al-Tirmidhi, Manaqib, 9)

Sometimes it may be necessary to repeat the word so that it can be understood well by the addressee. For this reason, important issues in the Qur'an are repeated several times in different chapters. For example,

Satan's disobedience to the divine command and not prostrating was repeated in seven places, and the situation of magicians who believed in Moses was repeated in four places.

While the Messenger of Allah – upon him peace and blessings - was leading the prayer, he would sometimes repeat the remarkable verses two or three times. In like manner, while giving advice and warning to the Companions, he would repeat some statements. It is possible to come across such repetitions in the conversations of the friends of Allah as well. However, repetition should be for the purposes of indoctrination. It should not cause boredom and should be appropriate for the level of the community.

2. It is strictly forbidden to make pretentious speeches with the intention of pedantry and to show oneself superior to others, or to address people with words that they cannot understand.

Now there is a kind of man whose views on the life of this world may please thee greatly, and [the more so as] he cites God as witness to what is in his heart and is, moreover, exceedingly skillful in argument. (al-Baqara, 2: 204)

Now when you see them, their outward appearance may please you; and when they speak, you are inclined to lend ear to what they say. [But though they may seem as sure of themselves] as if they were timbers [firmly] propped up, they think that every shout is [directed] against them. They

are the [real] enemies [of all faith], so beware of them. [They deserve the imprecation,] "May Allah destroy them!" How perverted are their minds! (al-Munafiqun, 63: 4)

Our beloved Prophet – upon him peace and blessings - said:

"Allah, the Exalted, hates the eloquent one among men who moves his tongue round (among his teeth), as cattle do." (Abu Dawud, Adab, 4987)

The Messenger of Allah never worried about the art in his speeches. Our beloved Prophet spoke with pure emotions, full of compassion and mercy, and with the most natural expressions of his soul.

3. One should not speak loudly by shouting. It is not right for a person to shout as if he is talking to the deaf or to speak in an angry tone as if he is fighting. Adopting a polite and gentle style is always the most appropriate way of speaking. As stated in the Qur'an, Luqman – upon him peace - recommended the method in question to his son as follows.

"And (O my son!) be moderate in your pace, and lower your voice; for the harshest of sounds without doubt is the braying of the ass." (Luqman, 31: 19)

When sending Musa and his brother Harun to Pharaoh, Allah wanted them to warn him with a gentle speaking, and ordered the use of a beautiful style as a matter of etiquette, even if the addressee is an unbeliever:

"Go, both of you, to Pharaoh, for he has indeed transgressed all bounds; But speak to him mildly; perchance he may take warning or fear (Allah)." (Ta Ha, 20: 43-44)

Kind words and the covering of faults are better than charity followed by injury. Allah is free of all wants, and He is Most-Forbearing. (al-Baqara, 2: 263)

4. It is forbidden for two people to whisper among themselves, excluding the third person with them. The Messenger of Allah said:

"When you are three, do not let two of you whisper in front of the other until they mingle with other people, doing so may cause distress to the lonely person."

"In most of their secret talks there is no good. However, secret conversations made by those who encourage giving alms, doing good or making peace between people are exempt from this. Whoever does this for the sake of Allah, We will certainly give him a great reward." (al-Nisa, 4: 114)

5. If any issue is being discussed in an assembly or if a question is asked to be answered, the right to talk first belongs to the elder of the assembly.

However, other people can also express their opinions in an appropriate manner if need be. As a matter of fact, when Abdurrahman bin Sahl, who is the youngest, first started to talk about an incident, our Prophet said; *"Leave the word to the elders, leave the word to the elders!"* Then the elders conveyed the story.

6. One should speak concisely and avoid unnecessary details. In other words, it is necessary not to talk much, but to speak appropriately and in moderation. This is one of the characteristics of a believer.

"Those who turn away from vain talks and deeds." (al-Mu'minun, 23: 3)

"But there are, among men, those who purchase idle tales, without knowledge (or meaning), to mislead (men) from the Path of Allah and throw ridicule (on the Path): for such there will be a Humiliating Penalty." (Luqman, 31: 6)

The Prophet -upon him blessings and peace- said:

"Do not talk too much without remembering Allah! Saying too many words other than the remembrance of Allah hardens the heart. There is no doubt that those with hard hearts are the furthest from Allah."

The Messenger of Allah -upon him blessings and peace- said:

"Every word of man is against him; except to enjoin good, forbid evil, or to remember Allah."

The Messenger of Allah -upon him blessings and peace- said:

"It is because of the goodness of a Muslim that he abandons what does not (directly) concern him."

7. Speeches that do not have any material or moral benefit, on the contrary, are harmful, should be strictly avoided. Our Almighty Lord states:

"Not a word does he (or she) utter, but there is a watcher by him ready (to record it)." (Qaf, 50: 18)

8. Saying "InshaAllah" when talking about the future is another etiquette related to speaking. To say "inshaAllah (If Allah wills)" when wishing for something for the future means to be aware of Allah's will and not to recognize a will above His will. As a matter of fact, it is stated in the Qur'an:

"And never say of anything, "I shall do such and such thing tomorrow." Except (with the saying), "If Allah wills!..." (al-Kahf, 18: 23-24)

MANNERS OF SPEAKING OVER THE PHONE

1- Introducing Oneself

The caller should politely introduce himself/herself before asking who the caller is.

2- Asking about availability

Before starting to talk, the person on the other side should be asked whether he/she is available to talk and then the caller should act accordingly.

3- Not prolonging the talk

The telephone is a means of communication. Therefore, very lengthy conversations should not be made over the phone. After greeting and briefly asking about the wellbeing, it is best to enter the subject, which is the purpose of the call, and then move on to the end of the talk.

4- Not interrupting

As in face-to-face conversations, one should not interrupt the other person's talk over the phone unless it is absolutely necessary. Those who talk on the phone should listen each other patiently and speak in turn. Utmost care should also be taken not to talk to a person over the phone and to another person next to you at the same time.

5- Not speaking too loudly

It is shameful and lack of good manners to talk too loudly on the phone in public areas. It is a disturbing behavior for both the person whom we talk over the phone and the people around you.

6- Not talking about private matters in front of others

Private matters, whether they are spoken face-to-face or over the phone, should be discussed in environments where others cannot hear. In addition, one should not let others to hear the voice of the other party without his knowledge.

7- Asking permission from the people with you

If your phone rings when someone is with you, you should either reject the call or before answering the call, ask the other person's permission. Because someone who comes to you in person is superior to someone who calls you over the phone. When you have someone with you, you should cut the phone call short out of respect. In addition, you should not play with the phone unnecessarily and surf the internet when someone is with you.

8- Coughing, sneezing, blowing nose while being over the phone

Do not sneeze, cough directly to the phone or wipe your nose in a way that may disturb the person whom you talk over the phone. You should apologize and ask for permission, and then minimize the disturbing sound by turning your head.

9- Not prolonging the dialing

If the other party's phone rings 3 or 4 times and does not pick it up, you should hang up and end the call. Because it is obvious that the other party is not available. You should not be calling again anytime soon. The person you are calling will get back to you when he/she sees your call.

10- Returning to missed call

You must certainly return to the missed calls. Because not returning to them indicates that you are not taking the other person seriously.

11- Not making calls too early in the morning or too late in the evening

Unless there is an emergency, it is important to try not to call too early in the morning and too late in the evening, that is, before 09:00 AM in the morning and after 21:30 PM in the evening.

12- Turning down the ringtone when necessary

In environments such as schools, mosques, cinemas, meetings, presentations and funerals, it is necessary to set the phone to silent mode.

13- Ending the call

The talk over the phone should not be ended abruptly, but rather by expressing good wishes.

14- Hanging the phone first by the caller

Whoever picks up the phone hangs up first. However, if you have talked to your elder or superior, you should not turn it off before your elder or superior does. In addition, telephone calls to the superiors in the workplaces should not be made through the secretary or the operator.

....

....

....

....

....

....

....

....

....

....

....

....

....

....

....

....

....

....

....

....

....

www.ingramcontent.com/pod-product-compliance
Lightning Source LLC
Chambersburg PA
CBHW062139160726
48282CB00027B/875
9789366084541